The Economics of Crime

D0223576

Since Gary Becker's seminal article in the late 1960s, the economic analysis of crime has blossomed, from an interesting side field within law and economics, into a mature stand-alone subdiscipline that has been embraced by many well respected academic economists. Wide-ranging and accessible, this is the most up-to-date textbook on the subject, taking current economic research and making it accessible to undergraduates and other interested readers. Without using graphs or mathematical equations, Winter combines theory and empirical evidence with controversial examples from the news media. Topics discussed include:

- the death penalty
- racial profiling
- rational drug addiction and drug legalization
- private crime deterrence
- gun control
- the privatization of prisons
- juvenile crime
- alternative social reforms to deter crime.

By requiring no previous knowledge of economics, not only is this book a perfect choice for students new to the study of economics and public policy, it will also be of interest and accessible to students of criminology, law, political science, and other disciplines involved in the study of crime topics. By emphasizing the benefits *and* costs of social policy to deter crime, *The Economics of Crime* can be enjoyed by anyone who follows current public policy debate over one of society's most contentious issues.

Harold Winter is Associate Professor at Ohio University. His previous book *Trade-offs: An Introduction to Economic Reasoning and Social Issues* is available from University of Chicago Press (2005).

The Economics of Crime

An introduction to rational crime analysis

Harold Winter

Routledge
Taylor & Francis Group

LONDON AND NEW YORK

First published 2008
by Routledge
2 Park Square, Milton Park, Abingdon, Oxon OX14 4RN

Simultaneously published in the USA and Canada
by Routledge
270 Madison Avenue, New York, NY 10016

Routledge is an imprint of the Taylor & Francis Group, an Informa business
© 2008 Harold Winter

Typeset in Times New Roman by Keyword Group Ltd

Printed and bound in Great Britain by Biddles Ltd, King's Lynn, Norfolk

British Library Cataloguing in Publication Data
A catalogue record for this book is available from the British Library

Library of Congress Cataloging in Publication Data
A catalog record for this book has been requested

ISBN 10: 0-415-77173-0 (hbk)
ISBN 10: 0-415-77174-9 (pbk)

ISBN 13: 978-0-415-77173-3 (hbk)
ISBN 13: 978-0-415-77174-0 (pbk)

To the professors who have influenced my thinking,
and to the students I have influenced.
You all know who you are.

Contents

Preface

The field of study known as the *economics of crime* is generally considered to have started with Nobel Prize winner Gary Becker's seminal article published in 1968. When I first read Becker's article in 1982, the economics of crime was an interesting subfield in the larger field of the economics of law, itself only a small field in the discipline of economics. Now, however, the economics of crime has matured into a stand-alone field that has been embraced by many well respected academic economists. And while anti-crime policy is one of society's "big" social issues, widely debated in the media by politicians and by concerned individuals, it is not often that the economic approach to crime is brought into the forefront of the debate. You may think of asking an economist about the unemployment or inflation rate, or about the balance of international trade, but would you ask an economist to voice a professional opinion on the death penalty, racial profiling, or drug addiction?

When I tell people I am writing a book on the economics of crime, the most common response I get is: What does economics have to do with crime? Well, economists have a lot to say about crime (and almost every other subject, for that matter). Currently, there exists a substantial body of scholarly work that is accessible primarily only to the scholars themselves. My main goal is to make some of this material accessible to a wider audience, creating a pedagogical tool for a topic in which there appears to be wide interest among students and others.

This book is primarily targeted at students who are not economics majors, or for those who have little background in economics yet may be taking an economics issues or contemporary problems course. There are several disciplines that routinely focus on crime topics, such as sociology, public policy, and, of course, criminology. If professors in these courses want to offer their students an introduction to the economic approach to crime, there is little material to use that may not be intimidating to the students. My book highlights the way economists think about a controversial social issue such as crime, and presents the material in a succinct, easy-to-read, and (hopefully) enjoyable format.

The main emphasis of my approach is to focus on the types of questions that economists raise. Economists have a way of identifying trade-offs that are not often considered by academics in other disciplines. Even though many of the theoretical economic models of crime are quite technical, there is always an intuitive core that can be pulled out and presented in an accessible manner. I plan not to shy away from some of the most difficult ideas, nor from some of the most controversial ones.

But regardless of how unique and interesting are the theoretical issues, there is also a large body of empirical work on the economics of crime. Generally, the important debates over empirical work do not really involve the opposing results of the studies. Instead, the debates primarily focus on the choice of data and statistical techniques. To fully appreciate these issues, the reader has to have some training in statistical analysis. With such a background, discussing how empirical studies differ can be an important and fascinating exercise. I'm going to assume, however, that the typical reader of this book does not have such a background.

Even with a strong background in statistics, the substantial lack of consensus among empirical researchers can be overwhelming not only to students, but also to academics. For example, while there is a strong consensus among economists over the underlying theory behind the deterrent effect of the death penalty, there are extremely well respected scholars who greatly differ over the empirical verification of the theory. This is simply the nature of applying empirical analysis to complicated real-world social issues. But the reasons for this lack of consensus can be poorly understood by students or lay people. Thus, they may incorrectly infer that there is little value in applying economic reasoning to crime issues.

I believe that readers who are fairly new to economic reasoning can be best served by being presented with concepts that offer the greatest consensus among economists, such as the notion of trade-offs. When I do discuss empirical studies, I focus on *what* the researchers are examining as opposed to *how* they are examining it. When I discuss empirical results, I usually emphasize the *qualitative* results over the *quantitative* results, but oftentimes present both, depending on the issue at hand. Furthermore, I do not present the results of any individual study as being definitive, only as being illustrative of the type of questions economists are trying to answer with empirical analysis. In Chapter 1 I provide a brief primer on empirical analysis to aid the reader in dealing with some of the empirical studies I discuss more formally. Professors who want to add more empirical content to the topics I discuss can easily do so with other readings that will complement my book. I include extensive references of papers I discuss and do not discuss in the text for the interested reader to pursue.

To maintain accessibility, in presenting the material I use no graphs, no math, few statistics, and a few numerical examples when needed for ease of exposition. This book is meant to be a *supplemental* text, offering students a short but serious discussion of the key topics in the economics of crime. Nearly every topic I discuss has been dealt with in book form, so I make no claim to have covered these topics exhaustively. Furthermore, there are many economics of crime topics I simply do not discuss at all. But, to the best of my knowledge, unlike any other book, this book makes accessible a substantial and up-to-date body of economic research. Finally, throughout this book I do not take sides in any specific debate, and I offer no explicit policy advice. My own opinion about any of the issues I discuss is of no relevance here. Although the ultimate goal of policy analysis is to answer questions about how to resolve social issues, I primarily want to focus on the first step toward that goal – raising the appropriate questions about trade-offs.

One last note for professors who are thinking about adopting this book for their course. Several reviewers of this book have suggested that it would be a more useful pedagogical tool if I offered comparisons between the economic and criminology approaches to crime issues. One early reviewer went so far as to suggest that I make such comparisons to demonstrate that economics offers a "better" approach to crime issues. My problem with that comment is that I don't believe economics offers a better approach – it is simply a *different* approach, nothing more, nothing less. I have always contended in my writing and my teaching that economic reasoning presents *a* way of thinking about public policy issues, not *the* way. It may be the way I personally think about public policy issues but, after all, I am a professional economist.

Another reviewer felt that I was not giving criminologists their due. By leaving out any discussion of criminology research I was ignoring important contributions made by criminologists, including many insights that were put forth long before economists reached similar conclusions. I admit that I am not addressing crime from a criminology perspective, nor from a psychology, political science, legal, or any other perspective. I appreciate that there is a tremendous overlap between the disciplines, each having interesting and unique perspectives to add. But, quite frankly, I lack the expertise in all of these other fields to discuss them in any credible fashion. It was a difficult enough task reading through the phenomenal economic literature on crime. I wouldn't even know where to start with all of the other fields. In short, this book focuses on economic reasoning only. If you are a criminology professor, or a professor in any other discipline, I hope this text allows your students to gain some insight into the economic approach to crime, and gives you the opportunity to address the sense (or nonsense) of that approach relative to your own.

H.W.

Acknowledgments

My main debt of gratitude goes to Robert Langham at Routledge. His interest in this project, and the encouragement he provided, were without bounds. For the excellent copy editing services they provided, I thank Abigail Humphries and Ray Offord. I also thank Thomas Sutton, Katherine Carpenter, and the many others at Routledge who made this a hassle-free and enjoyable project for me.

Throughout the past few years, I have had numerous students provide research assistance for me on this project. I thank Meghan Carter, Laura Kolat, Lindsey Lighthizer, Thomas McAdams, Emily Miner, Thomas Ruchti, Chris Sperry, and Adam Stohs, I hope I didn't forget anyone, but I apologize if I did. I also thank the students who took my crime course the first time I taught it. They provided me with many examples that appear in this book, and they put up with me as I stumbled through some of the material.

Finally, I'd like to thank my family for their constant encouragement and support. They get as big a kick out of these books as I do. And a special thanks to my wife Jenn, for not only providing her usual highly enthusiastic support, but also for providing one example in the drugs chapter.

1 Rational crime basics

I'd like to introduce to you the economic analysis of crime by asking you the following question: Would you rather live in a society in which murders occur, or in a society in which murders never occur? This is a question that requires no expertise to answer, and there is no right or wrong answer because I am asking you to state a personal preference. So, how would you answer this question? Do you even have to think about your answer for more than a second?

I've asked many people this question, and I don't remember ever encountering a response in favor of a society in which murders occur. For me, however, I would prefer to live in a society in which murders occur. Actually, I would *much* prefer to live in such a society, and this is not because I am murderer, or a sadist, or uncaring about the human tragedies associated with murder. My response stems from one simple fact – I think about these issues using economic reasoning.

Evidence, and common knowledge, suggest that crime is not a rare occurrence in the United States. In 2005 there were 1,390,695 violent crimes (murder, rape, robbery, and aggravated assault) reported in the United States, for a violent crime rate of 469.2 per 100,000 population. There were also 10,166,159 property crimes (burglary, larceny, and auto theft) reported, for a property crime rate of 3,429.8 per 100,000 population. And specifically for the crime of murder, there were 16,692 murders reported in 2005, for a murder rate of 5.6 per 100,000 population (FBI Uniform Crime Reports, *Crime in the United States, 1986–2005*. See the appendix to this chapter for definitions of crime categories).

Maybe, in some utopian sense, it would be preferable to live in a murder-free world. But from a more pragmatic perspective, exactly what sort of society would we have to live in to drive the murder rate to zero? One approach would be to come close to living in the society depicted in George Orwell's novel *1984* in which every individual is perfectly monitored at all times. Alternatively, maybe there is some way to change the nature of potential murderers to make them not want to commit murder, such as through counseling or drug therapy. More uniquely, in the movie *Minority Report* (based on a short story by science fiction author Phillip K. Dick), the authorities are able to predict murders before they occur and thus are able to arrest *potential* murderers. While I lack the expertise to evaluate the merits of this last option, I did see a serious round table discussion on television claiming that this approach will be technically feasible within the next twenty to fifty years. I wish them the best of luck with that.

So, one problem with trying to reduce the murder rate to zero is that it is unlikely that it would be technically feasible to do so. But even if it were technically feasible, I would like to ask another question: Would it be *desirable* to do so? For example, let's assume that we can reduce the number of murders per year by 50 percent. Reducing the murder rate by that much would require a tremendous amount of resources. As a society, we'd have to spend more on apprehending and convicting murderers, as well as on punishing them. We would have to draw resources away from other social programs, such as defense, education, health care, maintaining infrastructure, and so on. In fact, it might require us to completely abandon many other social programs to achieve such a phenomenal reduction in the murder rate. Under these circumstances, it simply may not be desirable, even if feasible, to reduce the murder rate by 50 percent.

In thinking about crime from an economic perspective, I believe there are three fundamental concepts that generally distinguish economic reasoning from other approaches. The first, stemming from the above discussion, is that because it requires costly resources to deter crime, the *optimal amount of crime* from a social perspective is very likely to be positive. Economists generally don't view crime as something the world would be better off without. We understand that it would not be technically feasible to eliminate all crime and, even more important, it would not be desirable to do so because of the substantial resource costs associated with crime prevention. Economics is often described as being the study of the allocation of *scarce* resources, and crime is just one of the many social problems toward which we devote our limited resources. The key economic issues concerning the costs of reducing crime center around the amount of resources that should be devoted to fighting crime, and how these resources should be divided between the different branches of the criminal justice system such as the police, the courts, and prisons.

Offsetting these costs are the benefits of anti-crime policy in terms of reduced crime rates. The key issue here is whether crime is reduced because individuals who have committed criminal acts are caught, convicted, and punished, or also because potential criminals are *deterred* from committing criminal acts in the first place. This leads to the second concept. Economists typically assume that criminals are *rational* in the sense that they weigh the costs and benefits of their actions, and that crime can be deterred by policies that manipulate the probabilities of arrest and conviction, and that determine the severity of punishment. This concept is discussed in more detail later in this chapter.

While the first two concepts make up the core of the economic approach to crime (that is, rational crime analysis considers both the resource costs *and* the deterrence benefits of anti-crime policies), the third concept is more abstract and controversial. If criminals themselves benefit from committing crime, these benefits may be considered as a social *advantage* of crime. In other words, if we weigh a criminal's benefit against a victim's cost for a particular crime, and the benefit outweighs the cost, an economist may conclude that the crime is, on net, beneficial to society.

This concept is so alien to most people that I believe it provides an excellent starting point for a detailed discussion of the economic approach to crime.

The benefit of crime

When you were younger, did you ever dream of growing up and becoming a police officer? Well, I am now going to give you a brief opportunity to fulfill that dream. Pretend that you are a state trooper. Currently, your duty involves monitoring a stretch of highway that has a speed limit of 55 m.p.h. but often attracts drivers who tend to far exceed that limit. You are cleverly parked out of the obvious view of oncoming traffic, and you have your radar detector at the ready. All of a sudden, a car goes racing by in excess of 90 m.p.h., and you immediately leap into action. In a matter of minutes, you have the culprit pulled over to the side of the road.

At more than 35 m.p.h. over the speed limit, you are expecting to present the driver with a very expensive ticket. Furthermore, you want to make it clear to passing drivers that this stretch of highway should no longer be used for speeding, so you expect to take your time before allowing the driver to continue on his way. But as you confront the driver, you are in for a surprise. He informs you that his passenger is his pregnant wife who has just gone into labor, and he was speeding to get her to the hospital as quickly as possible. Now what would you do?

While you are pondering that question, let me slightly change the story. Assume that everything is exactly the same as above except for one detail: the driver gives you a different explanation for why he was speeding. Instead of rushing his pregnant wife to the hospital, the driver was rushing with his wife to his favorite restaurant to eat lunch. It seems that he only has an hour for lunch, yet his favorite restaurant is fifteen miles away. He would never have time for his favorite meal unless he exceeded the speed limit. You've heard every excuse for why you should not ticket a driver caught speeding, but this is a new one for you. Would you respond differently to this excuse than you would to the previous one?

I obviously can't say for sure how you would respond in each case and, more important, I have no idea how a real state trooper would respond. (Although if you look at websites devoted to excuses for getting out of tickets, pregnancy is considered to be one of the best.) Nevertheless, how you believe each situation should be handled can provide us with a starting point for thinking about crime from an economic perspective. It wouldn't surprise me if you would be unlikely to ticket the driver with the pregnant wife, but certain to ticket the driver rushing to lunch. But does it make sense to treat the two cases differently?

These two scenarios share something important in common. In both cases, the driver is exceeding the speed limit by over 35 m.p.h. Whatever risks are associated with that behavior – the chances of getting into an accident and the extent of the damage – they are going to be very similar regardless of *why* the driver was speeding. In other words, to put it into economic jargon, the *cost* of the bad behavior is unlikely to depend on the justifications for such behavior. Yet if you answered that you would treat the two cases differently, you must be taking into account something that goes beyond the cost associated with excessive speeding. My guess is that you are implicitly thinking about the *benefit* of speeding.

From a commonsense point of view, if you are going to accept an excuse for speeding, taking a pregnant wife to the hospital is a much better excuse than rushing to get to a favorite restaurant for lunch. Thus, you recognize that the benefit of speeding in one case is greater than the benefit of speeding in the other case. Furthermore, if you are willing to excuse the driver in one case but not the other, you also recognize that the benefit of speeding exceeds the cost of speeding in that one case only. Your approach to traffic control, then, is to ticket drivers who are caught speeding who cannot adequately demonstrate that the benefit of their behavior outweighs the cost.

By accepting the argument that the driver with the pregnant wife should be excused from getting a speeding ticket, you are, at least implicitly, making an extraordinary claim: *a criminal should not be punished if the benefit of committing the crime outweighs the cost of the crime*. Yet why would anyone, other than a criminal, be concerned with a criminal's benefit of committing a crime? Is it sound social policy to excuse criminals who can justify their actions from a cost – benefit perspective? You seem to think so, if you excused the driver and his wife. But I'm sure that you don't believe this thinking can be applied to crimes that are more violent in nature, such as armed robbery, rape, or murder. You may be willing to tolerate excessive speeding under certain circumstances, but you would never be willing to tolerate murder. Some economists, however, may be willing to count a violent criminal's actions as a social benefit.

Deciding on whether or not to punish based on the benefit a criminal receives may seem a bit strange, yet economists routinely include such benefits in their analyses. David Friedman, in his book *Law's Order*, eloquently states it this way:

> If instead of treating all benefits to everyone equally we first sort people into the deserving and the undeserving, the just and the unjust, the criminals and the victims, we are simply assuming our conclusions. Benefits to bad people don't count, so rules against bad people are automatically efficient.
>
> (Friedman, 2000, p. 230)

But from a pragmatic policy perspective, what does it really mean to say that we are going to take into account a criminal's benefit? Let's use a simple numerical example to illustrate a point.

Consider a crime that imposes a $10,000 cost upon society. If we think about this single crime in isolation, depending on our social policy objective we may want to devote no more than $10,000 in resources to deter it. Now assume that the criminal reaps a $7,000 benefit from committing the crime. If we count this $7,000 as a social benefit (after all, the criminal is a member of society), the *net* cost of the crime is only $3,000 (the $10,000 cost minus the $7,000 benefit). By counting the criminal's benefit, we may want to devote only up to $3,000 to deter the crime. Thus, if criminal acts have offsetting benefits, it may be desirable to devote fewer resources to crime deterrence.

Unfortunately, this simple policy conclusion may be very difficult to implement in the real world. In justifying fewer resources devoted to crime deterrence, could you ever imagine a politician calling for a study to measure the benefits a rapist or child molester reap from their crimes? And even if you are comfortable attempting to measure the benefits of crime (as most economists would be), there would be substantial technical impediments to developing accurate measurements. But economic reasoning can be pushed further here, and we can say something more specific about the pragmatic role of counting a criminal's benefit. We can argue that there is such a thing as *efficient* crime.

The concept of efficient crime is, at its core, fairly simple: if the benefit of a crime outweighs its cost, it may be in society's best interest to *encourage* that crime. For example, what if we change the numbers from above such that the criminal reaps a benefit of $12,000 instead of $7,000? Do we then actually *gain* $2,000 from the commission of that crime? The typical economist would answer yes, arguing that this is an example of an efficient crime – the $10,000 cost is outweighed by the $12,000 benefit. In debating social policy in this case, an economist may argue that no resources should be used to deter this crime. And while I argued above that it may not be desirable to deter all crime because of the resource costs that would be needed to achieve that goal, now I am making a different argument: it may be efficient for some crimes to occur *even if it is costless to deter these crimes.*

Believing that some crimes can be efficient is a way of thinking of the world that to many, especially at first blush, seems ridiculous. But maybe it's more a matter of semantics. For example, consider the following facts. In March, 2005, in Morrisville, Pennsylvania, a forty-one-year old woman was attacked by three other women. Before being completely overcome by her attackers, the victim was able to grab a steak knife and stab one of her attackers in the leg. The knife wound was serious, and the injured woman died. Is this an example of efficient murder?

In this case, the victim of the attack was not charged with murder because it was deemed that she acted in self-defense. The killing was not defined as a crime, and so it went unpunished. But why is self-defense not defined as a crime? It must be because in some situations, it is in society's best interest to allow one individual to kill another. We can choose not to call it a crime, or we can call it a crime in which the benefit of the crime outweighs the cost. Either way, the activity of self-defense is allowed, even encouraged, when necessary.

From a social policy perspective, then, in considering how to deal with a criminal's benefit from committing a crime there are two fundamental issues. The first involves *identifying* all the relevant trade-offs, and the second involves *weighing* the importance of each trade-off. These are two very different issues, yet the distinction between them can easily be overlooked.

That a criminal receives benefits from criminal activity is a fact, not an opinion. To explain why an individual undertakes *any* activity, there must be benefits associated with the activity. However, deciding whether the benefits a criminal receives should be traded off against the costs of criminal activity in deciding social policy is another matter. As expressed by Friedman, economists tend to be *inclusive* when considering which individuals "count" from a social perspective. But one can just as easily believe that a criminal's benefit should not count.

Deciding on what counts or does not count is a subjective matter. If you sincerely believe that it is wrong to base social policy partly on the benefits that accrue to criminals, that is your opinion. If you believe that benefits should be counted in some situations, but not in others, that too is your opinion. There is no such thing as a "correct" social objective. Being inclusive is *a* way of thinking about social issues, but it is not *the* way. What ultimately matters is this: What policy conclusions can be drawn from considering different social objectives?

If the benefits are not counted to offset the costs of crime, it is in society's best interest to devote more resources to fighting crime. If the benefits are counted, however, there is an offset to the costs of crime, implying that crime is not as serious a social problem. There are two completely different social objectives at work here – one considers crime to be more socially costly than the other. If you truly believe that the social cost of crime is higher than I believe it to be, the efficient crime deterrence policy for you is likely to use more resources than will the efficient crime deterrence policy for me. With different objectives, there are different optimal solutions.

Rational criminals

Let's take a trip back in time to the American Old West. Three bank robbers are holding up a bank and threatening the employees and customers at gun point. After the leader of the gang grabs all the money and heads for the door, one of the robbers points his gun at a teller and is about to shoot. Just at the last second, the leader of the gang slaps the arm of his partner and prevents him from killing the teller. The startled partner looks at the leader and asks, "Why did you do that? They hang us for murder the same as they hang us for robbing banks. Why leave any witnesses?" To that the leader replies, "The posse rides harder for murderers."

That clever verbal exchange takes place in a movie (unfortunately, one for which I can't remember the title). I think it is an inspired piece of screenwriting because it accurately depicts some very subtle trade-offs that criminals may consider when they are planning to commit crimes. It is obvious that criminals rob banks in order to steal money. But offsetting this financial benefit are the costs of bank robbery, such as purchasing weapons and tools, and incurring planning costs. Furthermore, and possibly most important, bank robbers must contend with the risk of being caught and punished.

Put yourself in the boots of the bank robber with the itchy trigger finger. You realize that, if you are caught, you will face the death penalty whether or not you kill the witnesses. Because the punishment for the less severe crime of bank robbery is the same as it is for the more severe crime of murder, you conclude that there is no additional *deterrent effect* dissuading you from committing murder. Actually, you reason that you have an incentive to go ahead and kill the witnesses, hoping that this will lower your chances of being convicted if you are caught. Punishing bank robbery with the death penalty may discourage some criminals from robbing banks, but it may encourage criminals who do rob banks to do so more violently.

The leader of the gang, however, adds another layer of complexity to the problem. While there are two forces enhancing the incentive to commit murder – the punishment is the same for bank robbery and murder, and live witnesses may increase the chance of conviction – the leader recognizes that the probability of being apprehended may also depend on the nature of the crime. He believes that the crime of murder may provide the posse with the incentive to track the murderers relentlessly, whereas the crime of bank robbery may lead the posse to give up after a short time. This is very sophisticated thinking, by both bank robbers. They recognize that punishment doesn't occur 100 percent of the time. Instead, they have partitioned the punishment into its two basic components: the *severity* of punishment, and the *certainty* of punishment.

The severity of punishment refers to the form of the ultimate sanction a criminal faces. A prison sentence or a monetary fine are two very common sanctions. The longer the prison sentence, or the larger the fine, the more severe is the punishment. There are a variety of other sanctions that can be used, ranging from less severe punishments such as probation or community service, to more severe punishments such as torture or the death penalty. The certainty of punishment takes into account the probabilities of apprehension and conviction. To manipulate these probabilities, the authorities can, for example, hire more police officers, use more sophisticated investigation techniques, devote more resources to prosecuting cases, and so on. Regardless of how severe a punishment is, to be enforced it requires the criminal to be apprehended and convicted.

To effectively measure punishment, then, we need to take into account both its certainty and its severity. For example, assume that a criminal faces a 50 percent chance of being apprehended *and* convicted of a crime. Furthermore, assume that the sanction is a monetary fine of $1,000. However, the criminal does not simply face a $1,000 punishment. Instead, the criminal faces an average or, what economists refer to as, an *expected punishment* of (50 percent)($1,000), or $500. Notice that the criminal is never actually punished by the exact amount of $500. The sanction will either be $1,000 or nothing. But because the sanction is not incurred with certainty, the criminal confronts only an expected punishment that is less than the actual sanction.

Perhaps a more intuitively pleasing way to think about the expected punishment is to consider a criminal who repeatedly undertakes an illegal activity and faces a 50 percent chance of a $1,000 punishment each time. With every undertaking of the illegal activity, the criminal will *either* pay a fine of $1,000 or face no sanction at all. Over many periods of time, however, the $1,000 fine will be incurred in 50 percent of the periods, and not incurred in the rest of the periods. *On average*, then, the per-period fine is $500, even though the criminal never pays an actual fine of $500.

Returning to the Old West bank robbers, what the two criminals disagree about is the magnitude of the expected punishment. They both recognize that the ultimate sanction they face is the death penalty, but one believes they face a lower certainty of being punished if the witnesses are killed. The other, however, believes they face a higher certainty of punishment if the witnesses are killed. Regardless of who is correct, it is this concern over both the certainty and the severity of punishment that is at the core of rational crime analysis. To put it succinctly, economic models of crime predict the following: an increase in the expected punishment lowers the crime rate, while a decrease in the expected punishment raises the crime rate.

A rational criminal is assumed to weigh the costs and benefits of committing a crime, and commit the crime only if the benefits exceed the costs. Thus, criminals respond to changes in their environment – if it becomes more costly to commit crime, less crime will be committed. It is important to keep in mind, however, that rational crime analysis does not require all, or even most, criminals to behave with an explicit understanding of the expected punishment they face. Individuals who commit spontaneous crimes of passion, or individuals who are intoxicated, may not (at the moment the crime is committed) be too concerned with the expected punishment they face. There also may be individuals who are poorly informed about the expected punishment they face and possibly grossly underestimate it. There may even be individuals who, perversely, do not consider the expected punishment to be a cost. For example, in some violent street gangs, "serving time" may be considered a badge of honor, or part of an initiation process. It is easy to imagine that many criminals may not respond to changes in the expected punishment.

For rational crime analysis to have merit, all that matters is that *some* criminals take into account the expected punishment they face. If this is true, in pursuing a social policy to deter crime the authorities can affect the crime rate by manipulating the components that make up the expected punishment. Notice that rational crime analysis does not require us to know exactly *why* criminals commit crimes. The psychological and socioeconomic aspects of criminal behavior raise interesting and important questions, and the more we know about this behavior the better we will be able to reduce crime. But the driving force behind rational crime deterrence policy is that crime can be reduced by increasing the expected punishment, *regardless* of why criminals behave the way they do.

While it may appear to be simple common sense to believe that harsher punishment can have a dampening effect on the crime rate, ultimately it is an empirical issue. There are many empirical economic studies on the deterrent effect of punishment, especially in terms of the severity of punishment through prison sentences and the death penalty. These studies will be covered in detail in Chapters 3–4. For now, for ease of presentation, I am going to provide a brief introduction to empirical analysis by using a simple example that does not involve the economics of crime. Afterwards, I will discuss several empirical crime studies, primarily focusing on the deterrent effect of the certainty of punishment.

Interlude: A brief primer on empirical analysis

Let's say you want to conduct an empirical study to compare the annual salaries of high school teachers in the state of New York versus those in the state of New Jersey. You collect data on 100 teachers in each state, and calculate a simple average. You find that the average salary in New York is $2,000 higher than the average salary in New Jersey. You conclude that New York high school teachers are better paid than their New Jersey peers. Based on the limited information you have, this is a sound conclusion. But what other information may be useful to your study?

As of now, the only information you have to explain the difference in salaries is the state in which each teacher is employed. But a teacher's salary may depend on many other factors, such as: number of years of experience; number of years of education; public or private school teacher; inner-city or suburb teacher; grade level taught; subject taught; age; gender; race; union status; and, possibly, several others. Perhaps your finding is largely explained by the fact that, in your sample, the New York teachers have more years of experience than their New Jersey counterparts. This may be important information to consider.

Now assume that you can collect all the relevant data discussed above. With these data, you can use *regression analysis* to estimate your model. At its most basic, when you estimate a simple regression equation you are able to isolate the effect you are interested in studying. With the salary example, you can now distinguish between the salaries of New York and New Jersey teachers by *controlling* for all other variables. In other words, this statistical technique, in a sense, forces all the other variables to be identical for the teachers, and can just focus on the state in which the teacher is employed. If you find that New York teachers still have a larger annual salary than New Jersey teachers, you can say that their salary is larger with *all else equal*. That is, the difference in salary cannot be explained by differences in any of the other variables that are being controlled for in the regression equation. Furthermore, with a single regression equation, you can also isolate any other effect you are interested in studying. For example, you can determine the effect of gender on salaries, *all else equal*, or the effect of race on salaries, *all else equal*, or the effect of years of experience on salary, *all else equal*, and so on. Thus, a simple regression can yield a lot of information.

When presenting the regression results for a specific variable of interest, it is common for researchers to discuss the *sign* of the effect (positive or negative), the *magnitude* of the effect (large or small in an absolute sense), and, most important, the *statistical significance* of the effect (typically, whether or not the magnitude is "different" from zero). For example, after controlling for all other variables, you may find that the effect on salary of teaching in New York as opposed to New Jersey is positive, that is, the New York teachers have higher salaries. Furthermore, you may calculate the magnitude of the difference to be equal to $1,000. But it is important to note that the $1,000 is only an average amount, that is, there is some statistical spread around that value. This means you may have to qualify your statement by saying something like you are *95 percent confident* that the average salary in New York is between $500 and $1,500 larger than the salary in New Jersey. In this case, you can say the salary in New York is significantly larger (in a statistical sense) than the salary in New Jersey, because the spread around the average does not include the amount zero. If the spread does include the amount zero (for example, $-\$1,000$ to $+\$3,000$), then your average result may be positive, but it would not be considered statistically significant.

The above discussion is meant to be as barebones as it can be. Its sole purpose is to allow me to comfortably use such terms as *control variables*, or *statistical significance*, when I discuss the results of empirical studies. In practice, however, empirical analysis can be extremely complicated and contentious. There are many different statistical methods that can be used to measure the same effect, and even technically sophisticated statistical tools are readily available to the typical researcher because of advances in computer hardware and software. Also, real-world data can be difficult to obtain or inaccurately measured. Furthermore, there may be alternative ways to measure the same variable, or there may be a question of which data are relevant. In all, there is room for much legitimate debate in empirical research.

In my opinion, the best empirical work deals openly with these shortcomings. Many authors allow their data to be shared by other researchers. This is very useful. Being able to have someone else independently replicate your results is the first step toward having confidence in the integrity of your data. The second step is to allow a battery of tests to check for the *robustness* of your results. How well do your results stand up to different statistical methodologies, or different data sets? To the extent that data cannot be shared, it is more difficult to verify results. This does not mean that the studies were done incompetently or dishonestly, it just means that fewer scholars get to really put the data through the ringer.

Finally, again in my opinion, no single empirical study can truly be definitive. It may even be impossible to consider a consensus body of empirical research as definitive. Empirical analysis of complicated real-world social issues always has to deal with the shortcomings of statistical techniques. Empirical work is important, but almost always contentious. This is the nature of empirical research, and does not reflect poorly on economic reasoning.

Empirical crime studies: An instructive example

To begin illustrating the empirical approach to the economics of crime, I am going to discuss a study published in 1991 (Grogger, 1991). The author uses a data set drawn from arrest records maintained by the California Department of Justice. The sample consists of nearly 14,000 individuals who were arrested at least once during the years 1984 to 1986. As a proxy for criminal activity (a difficult variable to measure accurately), the author uses the number of times an individual was arrested in 1986. Although this is far from a perfect proxy of criminal behavior (because the number of arrests also reflects the efforts of the authorities to apprehend criminals), the author openly acknowledges this inevitable shortcoming.

As for the control variables, it is common for empirical crime studies to divide them into three main categories – deterrence, economic, and demographic. From a deterrence perspective, criminal activity is predicted to be inversely related to the expected punishment a criminal faces. The author uses a variable that is defined as an individual's number of prior (to 1986) convictions divided by the number of prior arrests as a proxy for the probability of conviction, a component of the certainty of punishment. To account for the severity of punishment, a variable defined as the average length of prison sentence served since age eighteen is included.

In the economic control variable category, it is usually predicted that criminal activity is inversely related to legitimate labor market opportunities. The author proxies these opportunities with an employment variable (defined as number of quarters employed in 1986), and an income variable (defined as reported earnings in 1986). Finally, in the demographic control variable category, it is common in these types of studies to expect that criminal activity is more prevalent amongst minorities and youth. The author includes variables that take into account the race (African-American or not), the ethnicity (Hispanic or not), and the age (born in 1960 or 1962) of the individual.

As for the main results of the study, the author finds that an increase in the certainty of punishment (through the probability of conviction) provides a more effective deterrent than does an increase in the severity of punishment (through the length of the prison sentence). The employment variable does not appear to have a significant effect on arrests, but the income variable does, with a $100 increase in annual income leading to, on average, an approximately 1 percent reduction in the number of arrests (quantitatively, a large effect). Finally, the author finds that African-Americans and Hispanics are arrested 66 percent and 52 percent more often than whites, respectively, and that older individuals are arrested 14 percent fewer times than younger ones.

For each variable of interest, it is important to remember that the impact of that particular variable on the arrest rate assumes that all the other variables are controlled for in the regression equation. Furthermore, the results of this, or any, empirical study should not be interpreted as *proving* that these relationships exist. Instead, at best what can be said is that, *given* the author's data and statistical methodology, these are the results that are found. I like to think of the results of any particular empirical study as providing one more piece to a never-ending puzzle, in which the pieces oftentimes do not fit together very well. This will be seen more clearly when I discuss the empirical studies concerning the death penalty (Chapter 4) and gun control (Chapter 6).

Deterrence and the certainty of punishment

One way for the authorities to vary the certainty of punishment is to manipulate the probability of apprehension. A difficult crime deterrent effect to capture empirically is the effect of increasing the size of a police force on reducing crime. The prediction is obvious: more police, less crime. Unfortunately, it is likely that the reverse causation also exists: more crime, more police. In cities with high crime rates, there are likely to be large police forces. Furthermore, in response to what may be a growing crime rate, a city may hire more police officers. Thus, it is not difficult to empirically find a *positive* relationship between the size of the police force and the crime rate. To find a deterrent effect, then, the reverse causation between crime and the size of the police force must be sorted out.

One study (Levitt, 1997a) attempts to isolate the deterrent effect of an increased police force by looking at police hiring in fifty-nine cities (with populations of 250,000 or more during the full sample period of 1970 to 1992) during a mayoral or gubernatorial election year. In election years, incumbent candidates may be "tough on crime" and flex their muscles by hiring more police. It appears that this is exactly what happens, as the data show that, on average, the size of police forces remains constant in non-election years, but increases by approximately 2 percent in election years. What this suggests is that the increase in the size of police forces may not be attributed to an increase in crime during election years. Instead, the increase can be attributed to political forces. If this is the case, this is a perfect setting to separate out the deterrent effect from the reverse causation effect. While the results of the study demonstrate a negative relationship of the size of the police force on the violent crime rate, the effect is fairly small. The study concludes that there is a deterrent effect, but it is weak. Furthermore, a later study (McCrary, 2002) finds an error in the original study that suggests that even the weak results are not reliable. But the important contribution of the original study is that it offers a unique attempt to sort out the relationship between crime and police hiring.

The second study (Corman and Mocan, 2000) also tries to sort out the reverse causation between crime and the size of the police force. Here the authors use *high frequency* data (that is, the data use monthly as opposed to quarterly or annual observations). Their reasoning is that if it takes, for example, several months for the authorities to increase the size of the police force in response to increased crime rates, the monthly data will be better suited to pick up the *concurrent* effect of police activity on crime. In that short time, the causation between crime and the size of the police force is likely to run in one direction only – more police, less crime.

The authors find that an increase in the number of arrests in New York City between the years 1970 and 1996 leads to a decline in the number of robberies, burglaries, and automobile thefts. Similarly, an increase in the size of the police force leads to a decrease in robberies and burglaries. They also find that the police are able to substitute between the number of arrests and the size of the police force to enhance the efficiency of resource use. For example, between 1970 and 1980 the size of the police force in New York City decreased by approximately one-third, yet the number of felony arrests increased by 5 percent. This occurred because the number of arrests for misdemeanors and violations, the least serious crimes, decreased by 40 percent and 80 percent, respectively.

Another way for the authorities to vary the certainty of punishment is to manipulate the probability of conviction. One study (Atkins and Rubin, 2003) examines the deterrent effect associated with this probability. In 1961 the Supreme Court ruled (in *Mapp v. Ohio*, 367 U.S. 643) that in state criminal trials, evidence that was obtained by the police illegally, that is, in violation of the

Fourth Amendment, was to be excluded. This has become to be known as the *exclusionary rule*. From a rational crime perspective, to the extent that the exclusionary rule makes it more difficult for the police to investigate crimes, or for prosecutors to convict defendants, criminals may face a smaller expected punishment and commit more crimes. The study takes advantage of the fact that prior to the Supreme Court ruling, of the forty-eight continental states, exactly half had already adopted some form of the exclusionary rule, while the other half had not. Because of this difference, it can be predicted that the crime rates in the states that already adopted a form of the exclusionary rule should not be affected by the Court's ruling. The other states, however, that would have to adopt the exclusionary rule, may face higher crime rates.

The study finds that in the states affected by the Court's ruling, crime rates did indeed increase. They find that, on average, the crime rate for larceny increased by 3.9 percent, for auto theft by 4.4 percent, for burglary by 6.3 percent, and for robbery by 18 percent. Focusing on suburban areas only, the effects were even larger, as violent crimes increased by 27 percent and property crimes increased by 20 percent. They interpret their results as implying that changes in criminal procedure can have a serious impact on crime rates, suggesting that there are offsetting costs to whatever benefits are associated with enhancing defendants' rights.

Taken together, what the above studies illustrate is that there is evidence that the authorities can manipulate the probabilities of arrest and conviction and affect the crime rate. In Chapters 3–4 I will discuss evidence that suggests that manipulating the severity of punishment can also affect the crime rate. The authorities, then, have many options to consider in setting the expected punishment. At first blush, it may seem that if we think of crime as being bad, we should consider setting a high level of expected punishment to deter as much crime as possible. But, from an economic perspective, there are more complicated trade-offs to consider.

Returning to the three key concepts of the economic approach to crime, when trying to set a desired expected punishment for a particular crime economists typically consider: the cost imposed on society by the criminal act; the benefit to the criminal of committing the act; the cost of the resources used to maintain the expected punishment. The relationship between each of these three things and the desired expected punishment is straightforward. The desired expected punishment for a particular crime should be greater the more costly is the crime, the less benefit there is to committing the crime, and the less costly the resources used to maintain the expected punishment. Quite simply put, the expected punishment should be set based on a consideration of the costs and benefits of crime deterrence.

For example, consider the crime of speeding once again. The more dangerous we believe speeding to be in terms of injuries and lives lost the greater should be the expected punishment. To the extent that we believe some drivers exceed the speed limit for valid reasons the lower should be the expected punishment, because this benefit of speeding mitigates some of the cost of speeding. Finally, if there is a technological change that makes enforcing the speeding laws less costly (such as digital photography that allows accurate detection of speeding with fewer resources devoted to manpower), the greater should be the expected punishment.

It should also be emphasized that, when thinking about crime deterrence from an economic perspective, it is possible to think about crime possibly being not only underdeterred, but also *over* deterred. As I discussed earlier in this chapter, no matter how heinous the crime, the *optimal* amount of crime is extremely likely to be positive. This is not to be confused with believing that crime is a good thing. But, because we live in a world of scarce resources, it will be too costly to deter all crime. Every dollar spent on crime deterrence will be one dollar less spent on something else. Eventually, we will get to a point where one more dollar spent on crime deterrence will be less effective than one more dollar spent elsewhere. Thus, as a society, it is possible to spend *too much* on crime deterrence. The next chapter addresses the issue of how best to use resources to achieve a desirable level of crime deterrence.

Appendix: Definition of crimes

Murder.   The willful (non-negligent) killing of one human being by another.

Forcible rape (Sexual assault).   The carnal knowledge of a female forcibly and against her will. Assaults or attempts to commit rape by force or threat of force are also included; however, statutory rape (without force) and other sex offenses are excluded.

Robbery.   The taking or attempt to take anything of value from the care, custody, or control of a person or persons by force or violence and/or by putting the victim in fear.

Assault (Aggravated assault).   The unlawful attack by one person upon another for the purpose of inflicting severe or aggravated bodily injury. (This type of assault is usually accompanied by the use of a weapon or by means likely to produce death or great bodily harm.)

Burglary.   The unlawful entry of a structure to commit a felony or theft. (The use of force is not required to classify an offense as burglary.)

Larceny (Theft).   The unlawful taking, carrying, leading, or riding away of property from the possession or constructive possession of another. It includes such crimes as shoplifting, pocket-picking, purse-snatching, thefts from motor vehicles, thefts of motor vehicle parts or accessories, bicycle thefts, etc., in which no use of force, violence, or fraud occurs. (This crime category does not include embezzlement, confidence games, forgery, and worthless checks. Motor vehicle theft is a separate category.)

Motor vehicle theft.   The theft or attempted theft of a motor vehicle, includes the stealing of automobiles, trucks, buses, motor cycles, motor scooters, snowmobiles, etc.

Crimes against persons (Violent crimes).   Total of all crimes of homicide, forcible rape, robbery, and aggravated assault.

Crimes against property.   Total of all crimes of burglary, larceny-theft, and motor vehicle theft.

Notes

The seminal paper on the economics of crime is by Becker (1968). Several good overview papers on the topic are by Cameron (1988), Ehrlich (1996), DiIulio (1996), Garoupa (1997), Eide (1999), and Polinsky and Shavell (2000). Two interesting books on the economics of crime are by Sieberg (2005) and Cohen (2005). The book by Friedman (2000, chapter 15) also offers an introductory discussion.

Empirical studies on the deterrent effect of various components of expected punishment are by Viscusi (1986), Grogger (1991), Tauchen, Witte and Griesinger (1994), Levitt (1997a), but see the rebuttal by McCrary(2002) and the reply by Levitt (2002), Corman and Mocan (2000, 2005), Atkins and Rubin (2003), DiTella and Schargrodsky (2004), and Lee and McCrary (2004). Non-empirical papers on the deterrent effect are by Shavell (1987a, 1989), Friedman and Sjostrom (1993), Mookherjee and Png (1994), Bar-Gill and Harel (2001), and Robinson and Darley (2004) who offer a thoughtful, skeptical view on the existence of the deterrent effect.

2 Efficient punishment and fines

Consider the following novel approach to deterring speeding on state highways. In each state, there will be just a handful of unmarked police cars to enforce the speed limit. If you are caught speeding, you must immediately forfeit your vehicle, all the money you are carrying, and any other property you have with you. You will never be imprisoned, and you will face no further punishment other than having a long walk home.

Although this sounds like a ludicrous way to enforce the speeding laws on state highways, and it is never going to seriously be considered in the real world, at its core there is a strong economic soundness to this policy option. By using only a handful of police cars, the authorities are imposing a very low *certainty* of punishment. But by applying a large sanction to those drivers who are caught speeding, the authorities are imposing a very high *severity* of punishment. In other words, if you enjoy speeding on the state highways, it is very unlikely you will ever be pulled over. But if you are pulled over, beware – you will be severely punished. Thus, even with a low probability of being caught, the expected punishment may still be large enough to deter speeding. This may be a sound social policy because the authorities are using very few resources to achieve their goal. And, to an economist, the fewer resources used to achieve a specific goal, the better.

Certainty versus severity of punishment

A substantial challenge in setting a desired expected punishment is to determine the appropriate trade-off between the certainty and severity of punishment. For any level of expected punishment that can be set, there are many combinations of certainty and severity that yield the identical expected punishment. The authorities have to consider how to *simultaneously* set the probabilities of apprehension and conviction, as well as choose an appropriate sanction. To sort through these combinations, economists rely on a simple premise: for any desired level of expected punishment, choose the combination of certainty and severity that uses the *least* amount of resources. With an efficiency objective stated, the task now becomes to achieve that objective. Toward this end, economists typically recommend doing two things: use the sanction of fines as often as possible; and, combine a low certainty of punishment with a high severity of punishment.

When comparing fines and prison sentences, two of the most common forms of sanctions, sustaining a system of fines is likely to require far fewer resources than needed to sustain a prison system. Prisons are typically very costly to build and maintain. Fines, on the other hand, are rather simple to set – choose a monetary amount for the fine and then require the defendant to pay that amount. Of course, resources will be needed to administer and enforce fines, but this will likely be a modest amount of resources when compared to those needed to administer and enforce prison sentences.

If the sanction of fines is being used, for any desired expected punishment the next step is to determine the optimal combination of certainty and severity of punishment. For example, let's return to the numerical example I used in Chapter 1 and assume that the desired level of expected punishment is $500. One combination of certainty and severity that achieves that outcome, as seen before, is to set the certainty at 50 percent and the fine at $1,000 for an expected punishment of (50 percent)($1,000), or $500. But that is not the only way to set the expected punishment at $500. The authorities can set a larger fine of $5,000 and a smaller certainty of 10 percent, or a smaller fine of $750 and a larger certainty of approximately 67 percent, or many other combinations. But to maintain a constant level of expected punishment, the certainty and severity of punishment must move in *opposite* directions.

How can the authorities determine the optimal trade-off between the certainty and severity of punishment? One simple answer is to consider the relative costs of establishing the certainty and severity of punishment. To increase the probability of apprehending and convicting criminals, more resources will have to be devoted to enhance police and prosecutorial efforts. But, to increase a fine, all that is needed is to state a larger dollar amount. It is likely, however, that, as a fine gets larger, so will the enforcement costs of collecting that fine, but it isn't difficult to believe that the resource cost of enhanced certainty is likely to exceed the resource cost of enhanced severity. So, if we consider the three combinations that yield a $500 expected punishment – 67 percent of $750, 50 percent of $1,000, or 10 percent of $5,000 – the last option is likely to require the fewest resources to maintain.

If keeping the resource cost of setting the certainty of punishment low is a true goal, we can push the argument to its logical extreme. Why not make the probability of getting a ticket *very* low, say 0.1 percent (one in a thousand) and set the fine very high at $500,000? This combination of certainty and severity yields an expected punishment of (0.1 percent)($500,000), or $500, yet the resource cost of maintaining a certainty level of 0.1 percent is likely to be substantially lower than maintaining the level at 10 percent with a fine of $5,000. Using economic reasoning, then, the desired level of expected punishment should be set using a very low certainty of punishment with a very high monetary severity of punishment.

Yet in the real world, for most crimes we rarely observe huge fines applied with extremely low probabilities. Why is that?

The problems with fines

The first obvious problem with using very large fines is that most individuals would simply lack the ability to pay them. Getting a $500,000 fine for speeding would provide you with a great story to tell your friends at work the next day, but unless you were extremely wealthy it would have the same deterrent effect as a $400,000 fine, or a $200,000 fine. Thus, a 0.1 percent chance of being fined $500,000 would not actually lead to an expected fine of $500 because the $500,000 fine would be, in pragmatic terms, nonsensical. But the basic approach of combining a large fine with a low certainty of punishment can still hold true, if slightly revised: set fines as high as *pragmatically* possible, and increase the certainty of punishment only as much as needed to achieve the desired expected punishment. With the extreme approach to punishing speeding introduced above, few resources are used in the enforcement of the speeding laws. Furthermore, every individual caught speeding can "afford" to pay the fine because the fine is constrained by what the individual physically has on hand. The key, then, to using this approach appears to be to determine how many state troopers are needed to sustain the appropriate level of certainty of punishment.

Alternatively, the authorities can maintain a very low certainty of punishment, set fines as high as possible, and enhance the severity of punishment with prison sentences. This last option can be efficient if the resource cost of increasing the certainty of punishment is high relative to the cost of imprisonment. One study (Waldfogel, 1995) finds that, for fraud offenders, fines are directly related to a defendant's ability to pay and are used reasonably efficiently with prison sentences. On average, for each one-month reduction in the prison sentence, there is a $1,500–$2,000 increase in the fine. This suggests that, while monetary sanctions are not being used exclusively or excessively, they are being used on the margin to reduce the resource cost of imprisonment.

There are several other reasons why it may be inefficient to use excessive sanctions to deter crime, even when the sanctions require few resources to implement, such as with fines. One problem with a very harsh sanction is that it may encourage criminals to seriously attempt to evade capture. Imagine that you are driving along the highway a few miles over the speed limit and you have the misfortune to see one of the few state highway patrolmen pull out behind you. You realize that, if you are pulled over, you will lose everything you have with you. You may not be very cooperative at that point in time, and a dangerous high-speed chase may prevail. These chases can lead to property damage and personal injuries, possibly even loss of life, and all because you were speeding.

There is another potential problem with harsh punishment explicitly when sanctions take the form of fines or forfeiture of property. In these cases, not only are criminals punished by the sanction, the authorities explicitly profit from the sanction. An article in the *Columbus* (Ohio) *Dispatch* (August 6, 2005) discusses this phenomenon.

> [A] Columbus dope dealer got five years in prison. The federal government and state and local law-enforcement agencies got $840,190 of his money and a lot of his property – three cars, a tow truck, three all-terrain vehicles, a John Deere tractor, a speedboat, a Wave Runner and three trailers. The law-enforcement agencies sold most of the property and divided the proceeds and the cash among themselves. Under a 1984 law, federal law enforcement can take property used in pornography, white-collar or drug crimes as well as illegal profits and property bought with dirty dollars. Assets can be seized through court action even if the owners are never charged with a crime. "Take away what they've gained in crime and that reduces the incentive," said Fred Alverson, a spokesman for the U.S. attorney's office in Columbus.

While it is true that if you reduce the gain from crime you reduce the incentive to commit crime, by allowing the state to take property you also increase the authorities' incentive to catch criminals. And, surprising as it may sound, giving the authorities more incentive to catch criminals may be inefficient.

For example, you often hear about a small town that is famous for the "speed trap" along a stretch of highway that goes through its jurisdiction. Because speeding tickets are a way of generating revenue, the police may have an incentive to catch a lot of individuals who speed by strictly enforcing the speeding laws. But why is this a problem? As long as the tickets are sincerely given to drivers who speed, only the guilty are punished.

The problem with excessive ticketing is that too many resources may be going toward deterring speeding just for the sake of the police trying to reap financial gain. Recall that the justification for setting a high severity of punishment is to save resources by simultaneously setting a low certainty of punishment. But if the authorities reap financial gains, they may have the incentive to use a high severity *and* high certainty of punishment. Also, resources may be drawn away from the investigation of other crimes that do not offer the authorities financial rewards, so there may be underdeterrence of those crimes and overdeterrence of speeding. Finally, financial gain to the police may give them an incentive to act corruptly by fining the innocent as well as the guilty, especially if those who have their property taken can retrieve their possessions only by suing the state. Thus, eliminating excessive financial sanctions may lead to more efficient crime deterrence policy.

There is yet another argument against using large fines with a low certainty of punishment. If the rational criminal is concerned only with the *level* of the expected punishment, and not how that level is made up of the two components, it can be argued that the choice of certainty versus severity can be based on their respective resource costs. If fines are relatively cheap to enforce, but maintaining a high level of probability of apprehension uses a lot of resources, a small certainty combined with a large severity of punishment will likely be efficient. However, it is possible that a criminal is not only concerned with the level of the expected punishment, but also with the magnitudes of the various components.

Let's look at a more realistic breakdown of an expected punishment that has three components – the probability of apprehension, the probability of conviction (given apprehension), and the severity of the punishment, in this case a monetary fine. Assume that the probability of arrest for a particular crime is 40 percent, the probability of conviction given the arrest is 80 percent, and the fine is $100,000. The expected punishment, then, is (40 percent)(80 percent)($100,000) = $32,000. If the criminal is only concerned with the $32,000 level of the expected punishment, it wouldn't matter how the three components are broken down, at least not for deterrence purposes. However, it is quite possible that each individual component of the expected punishment is not given equal weight by the criminal.

If we raise the probability of apprehension to 50 percent, don't change the probability of conviction, and lower the severity to $80,000 we still have an expected punishment of (50 percent)(80 percent)($80,000) = $32,000. Yet if the criminal is more sensitive to the change in the probability of apprehension than to the change in the severity, there may be a *greater* deterrent effect from the new numbers. Similarly, we can keep the probability of apprehension at 50 percent, return the severity to $100,000, and lower the probability of conviction to 64 percent to also maintain an expected punishment of (50 percent)(64 percent)($100,000) = $32,000. If the criminal is more sensitive to the change in the probability of apprehension than to the change in the probability of conviction, again there may be a greater deterrent effect compared to the original numbers. It may be that apprehension has more of an impact than conviction or severity because it is more immediately incurred by the offender. Arrest is simply the start of a chain of criminal justice events that may take weeks or months (or sometimes years) to be fully realized. Furthermore, as discussed below, apprehension in and of itself may be punitive if it imposes a social stigmatizing effect on the offender.

One study (Grogger, 1991, discussed in Chapter 1) finds that criminals do appear to be more sensitive to changes in the certainty of punishment relative to changes in the severity of punishment. The policy implications of this result can be substantial. It may be the case that a small expected punishment with a high probability of apprehension has a greater deterrent effect than a higher expected punishment with a low probability of apprehension. If this is true, by considering what component of the expected punishment criminals appear to be most sensitive to, it may be efficient to move resources away from conviction and severity and toward apprehension.

There are several other more subtle and technical arguments as to why a large fine combined with a low certainty of punishment may not realistically be an efficient way to set an expected punishment, but I'd like to make one more obvious, yet serious, point. Let's say the authorities decide to handle illegal parking by hiring very few officers and using extremely large fines. Even if few resources are needed to sustain this form of expected punishment, another problem may occur when a ticket is served: What next for the violator?

Bankrupting an individual who commits a crime may not require many resources, but it leaves an individual in grave financial trouble. Even if the expected punishment is reasonable, due to the low probability of receiving a ticket, there will be a small percentage of individuals who may now be a burden to the state or, even worse, decide to pursue more serious crimes. Typically, individuals who face even small probabilities of suffering large losses mitigate these risks by purchasing insurance, such as with life, home, and health insurance. Allowing individuals to purchase punishment insurance, however, would not be a good idea. "I think I'll rob a bank today. If I'm caught, and heavily fined, so what? I'm insured." Insurance companies would have no incentive to sell this type of insurance, and individuals would have to bear their own risks of incurring sanctions. This type of excessive risk placed on individuals, even criminals, may lead to further problems that would require substantial resources to resolve.

This particular problem with fines has led some scholars to argue that fines are a punishment best imposed against the wealthy because they are in the best position to be able to afford to pay the financial penalties without extreme hardship. But this raises the criticism that the wealthy and poor will be treated differently by the criminal justice system. Furthermore, if wealthy criminals are fined and not imprisoned, it is sometimes argued that this will encourage the wealthy to commit crimes as long as they feel that they can afford to pay the fines if caught. Imprisonment, on the other hand, is a harsher penalty and thus creates a greater deterrent effect. From an economic perspective, however, fines and imprisonment can lead to the same deterrent effect.

As with any punishment, the key is for the authorities to set the desired expected punishment by simultaneously choosing the certainty and severity of punishment. For example, consider the crime of stealing money. If a criminal's fine for stealing $1,000 is to pay a fine that is *less* than $1,000, there is no deterrent effect to that severity of punishment. If the fine is exactly $1,000, there is still little deterrent effect *unless* the certainty of being punished is 100 percent. In other words, if it is desirable to deter the crime of stealing $1,000, the *expected* punishment the criminal faces must be no less than $1,000. In this case, it is likely that, whatever the equivalent sanction is in terms of imprisonment to deter the theft of $1,000, the prison sentence will require more resources to enforce than will the fine, yet both forms of sanction can deter crime if set at the appropriate levels.

In using fines to deter corporate crime, a common criticism has been that, historically, the fines have been set at too low a level to offer any real deterrent effects. In 1991, the U.S. Sentencing Commission established sentencing guidelines to substantially increase the fines used against corporate offenders, and to lessen the discretion judges had in sentencing such offenders. Examining sentences imposed on publicly traded firms between the years 1988 and 1996, one study (Alexander, Arlen, and Cohen, 1999) finds that corporate fines did substantially increase after the guidelines were enacted. Prior to the guidelines, for the subset of cases they examine, they find the average fine to be approximately $1.9 million.

After the guidelines, the average fine is $19 million, representing a tenfold increase in criminal sanctions imposed on corporations. Another study (Parker and Atkins, 1999), however, examines a different subset of cases and finds that the guidelines had, at best, only marginal effects on the fines imposed on corporate criminals. The authors suggest that the guidelines may have been more of a political maneuver to promote a "tough on corporate crime" platform, without really having much of a real effect on corporate crime sanctions. Nevertheless, even these authors recognize that at least some corporate offenders faced substantially higher sanctions due to the guidelines.

While it is true that wealthy and corporate criminals may be underdeterred from committing financial crimes when the fines are inappropriately set, the solution to this problem is simply to carefully think about the desired level of expected punishment to enforce. A different criticism arises when the expected punishment is appropriately set yet some offenders *choose* to commit crimes, realizing they have to pay the fine only if caught and convicted. For example, consider the crime of double parking. Assume that, due to traffic congestion, each incidence of double parking imposes a $100 cost on society. If the authorities set the expected punishment for double parking at exactly $100, any individual who values double parking at an amount greater than $100 will commit the crime and be willing to pay the fine if caught. This suggests that wealthy individuals may easily be able to "get away" with double parking, while poor individuals may be deterred. But if this the case, from an economic perspective that may not be a problem. As discussed in the previous chapter, if a criminal's benefit of committing a crime is being counted as a social benefit, it is efficient for any criminal who values double parking at an amount greater than $100 to go ahead and double-park. For these individuals, double parking is an efficient crime. Still, to the extent that fines appear to be a sanction that suggests differences in how wealthy and poor defendants are treated by the criminal justice system, such sanctions will often be criticized as being unfair.

In all, while the idea to combine a low certainty of punishment with a high monetary sanction may be sound in theory, it suffers from several pragmatic problems. When a basic theoretical result does not hold up well to real world scrutiny, that does not imply that the result has no value. Quite the contrary. That particular result has tremendous value in economic models of crime because it presents an important *benchmark* on which to base other results. While that result is intuitively pleasing in the context of a theoretical model, economists can ask how the model can be refined to yield results that are intuitively pleasing in more of a pragmatic sense. Furthermore, sometimes the basic result can hold true in a slightly different context, as seen in the next section.

Shaming punishments

In one episode of the television show *The Practice*, a judge shames a Peeping Tom by having him take off his clothes from the waist down in open court. One would think that this ridiculous punishment can come only from the mind of a television screenwriter. In reality, however, shaming punishments are commonly used by judges:

> Shoplifters have been required to stand outside stores wearing signs announcing their crimes.
> A purse snatcher was ordered to wear noisy tap shoes in public.
> Drivers convicted of driving while intoxicated have been ordered to use special license plates that acknowledge their crime.
> Convicted sex offenders have been ordered to place signs on their front lawns that warn away children.
> A "slum landlord" was ordered to live in one of his rat-infested properties.

As another example, although I don't remember the specific details, in the mid 1980s I read about a community that tried an interesting experiment – they gave convicted nonviolent burglars a say in determining their punishment. They could either choose a jail sentence, or pay for a full page advertisement in the local newspaper. The ad would show their picture, describe their crimes, and offer an apology to their victims and the community. If I remember correctly, most of the criminals chose to serve time in jail. As a result, the community abandoned the program because it was deemed a failure. But maybe they should have placed a different interpretation on the lack of criminal interest in the newspaper ad. The fact that criminals did not choose the ad suggests that it was a more severe punishment to them compared to the jail sentence. Thus, the ad was likely to have more of a deterrent effect. Furthermore, from a resource cost perspective, the ad is virtually costless to impose. For an economist, it doesn't get much better than being able to devote fewer resources toward greater deterrence.

Although shaming punishments can be imposed on many types of criminals, supporters of such punishments generally believe they will be most effective against wealthy defendants, particularly white-collar criminals. For example, a convicted embezzler can be punished by having to write a letter of apology and publishing it in a professional trade magazine or widely read newspaper. This direct form of shaming may be extremely detrimental to the criminal's future reputation. Even if shaming punishments are not directly used, shame and other costs can be associated with arrest, conviction, and imprisonment due to a defendant's possible lost reputation, legal costs, inability to enjoy pre-arrest income, and difficulty in securing post-release employment. Furthermore, these additional costs are likely to be more substantial for a wealthy defendant than for a poor one.

One empirical study (Lott, 1992a) attempts to measure the difference between pre-conviction income and post-conviction earnings for criminals who have served time in prison for committing embezzlement or fraud. The largest reductions in legitimate income are found to occur for the wealthiest criminals. In fact, the author finds that even a modest increase in the offender's income (one standard deviation increase) can lead to a huge (fivefold) increase in the *total* monetary penalty (direct and indirect) faced by the criminal. This difficulty in returning to a pre-conviction level of income is due to the negative reputation effect associated with conviction.

Also, for several professions that require licenses to practice, disbarment often occurs due to the conviction. The author confirms this result in another study (Lott, 1992b) that looks at defendants convicted of drug offenses, and again finds that the wealthier the defendant the more severe is the total penalty associated with conviction. Another study (Waldfogel, 1994) examines the *persistence* of these negative conviction effects on employment and income, and concludes that the negative effects last for a long time (up to several years). On the other hand, one other study (Grogger, 1995), finds that arrests have only small effects on income and employment, and these effects are short-lived.

These low cost, high deterrence, forms of punishment may be efficient, but they are not without controversy. One criticism of shaming punishments is that the amount of shame a criminal incurs may vary greatly from person to person. I may find it awful to have to stand in front of a post office wearing a sign that reads: "I stole mail. This is my punishment" (an actual real-world punishment). Some people may actually get a kick out of doing that, especially when compared to being fined or imprisoned. Thus, it may be very difficult to gauge the deterrent effect of any particular shaming punishment. But this point is true for all forms of punishment. Different individuals respond differently to similar punishments, whether they are fines, imprisonment, or something else. In the next chapter I will discuss how a prison sentence of any fixed amount of time may not be an equally severe punishment to every individual.

Another criticism of low cost punishments, as discussed above, is that they appear to be unfair, or unjust, especially if they are more often applied to wealthy criminals rather than poor criminals. In the past few years, there has been a public backlash against white-collar criminals being fined rather than imprisoned for their crimes, even when large fines are used and they are coupled with career-ending negative publicity. So what if an embezzling CEO is fined into bankruptcy and prevented from ever being in that position again? Some people feel that harsher punishment is warranted.

It is not a matter of right or wrong to believe that fines or shaming punishments are inappropriate because they are not harsh enough. Instead, it depends on what your objectives are in setting punishment. In terms of deterrence and economic efficiency, if two punishments have equal deterrence, the one that requires the fewest resources to implement will be preferred. But to many, there may be a bit of a "Goldilocks" effect going on. Low resource cost punishments such as fines or shaming punishments may seem too soft, while others such as flogging or torture may seem too harsh. Yet a high resource cost punishment such as imprisonment may be just right. I discuss this widely used form of punishment in the next chapter.

Notes

Papers dealing with fines as sanctions are by Polinsky and Shavell (1979), Friedman (1981), Shavell (1991b) on specific versus general law enforcement, Waldfogel (1995) on the trade-off between fines and prison sentences, Levitt (1997b), Polinsky (2000), and Garoupa (2001).

Papers on corporate crime are by Karpoff and Lott (1993), Alexander and Cohen (1996, 1999), Cohen (1996), Lott (1996), Parker (1996), Ulen (1996), Alexander (1999), Alexander, Arlen and Cohen (1999), and Parker and Atkins (1999). An interesting paper on who are the corporate whistleblowers is by Dyck, Morse and Zingales (2007).

Papers on shaming punishments are by Kahan (1996), Rasmusen (1996), Kahan and Posner (1999), Owens (2000), and Funk (2004).

Papers on the reputational effects of arrest and conviction are by Lott (1992a, b), Waldfogel (1994), and Grogger (1995).

3 Prison and crime deterrence

Imprisonment is a common form of punishment for convicted criminals. There are several custodial jurisdictions in the United States, depending on whether the defendant is under the control of the federal (that is, national) authorities, the state (regional) authorities, or the local (city or county) authorities, as well as a few other jurisdictions. By the end of 2005, there were nearly 2.3 million individuals imprisoned in the United States. Approximately 1.3 million inmates were in state prisons, 748,000 were in local jails, 179,000 were in federal prisons, 96,000 were in juvenile facilities, and 30,000 were in territorial, military, immigration, or Indian country facilities. Stated another way, one in every 136 U.S. residents was incarcerated. In state prisons by the end of 2003, approximately 52 percent of the inmates were imprisoned for violent crimes (such as murder, manslaughter, rape, robbery, and assault), 21 percent for property crimes (such as burglary, larceny, auto theft, and fraud), 20 percent for drug crimes, and 7 percent for public order crimes (such as weapons charges, drunk driving, court offenses, and liquor law violations). In federal prisons by the end of 2003, 11 percent of the inmates were imprisoned for violent crimes, 7 percent for property crimes, 55 percent for drug crimes, and 27 percent for public order crimes (including immigration violations) (Bureau of Justice Statistics Bulletin, *Prisoners in 2005*).

As with fines, the threat of a prison sentence may lower the crime rate by deterring potential criminals from committing crimes. But, unlike fines, imprisoning criminals can also reduce the crime rate because of the *incapacitation effect*. Quite simply, an incarcerated prisoner can no longer commit crimes outside of the prison environment. Notice, however, that this explanation for crime reduction does not require the criminal to be deterred by the *threat* of punishment. Instead, it is the *actual* punishment of imprisonment that reduces the crime rate.

If incapacitation is the main force behind crime reduction, the authorities may want to consider *who* should remain incapacitated. For example, if older prisoners, or sickly prisoners, or possibly rehabilitated prisoners (if that can be determined) are very unlikely to commit further crimes upon release, there is little reason to keep them in prison. If deterrence is the main force behind crime reduction, shortening a prison sentence *after* incarceration leads to less of a threat of punishment *before* a crime is committed. A rational criminal is likely to be more concerned with the actual prison sentence that will be faced, as opposed to the announced sentence.

A thirty-year-old criminal who expects to be released by the age of forty is not going to be overly concerned with any threatened sentence that exceeds ten years. For deterrence purposes, then, the threat of a specific prison sentence must be believable.

To enforce prison sentences, a substantial amount of resources must be used. For example, in 2001 state prison operating expenditures totaled $28.4 billion, or $22,650 per inmate, or $100 per U.S. resident. Two-thirds of these expenditures were made up of salaries, wages, and benefits. Over a quarter of these expenditures were made up of basic living expenses, including prisoner medical care, food service, and utilities (Bureau of Justice Statistics Special Report, *State Prison Expenditures, 2001*). For these resources to be used efficiently, a distinction between the deterrent effect and the incapacitation effect of prison is an important one for the authorities to consider. First, I will consider the theoretical distinction between the two effects, then I will examine some of the empirical studies that attempt to isolate the deterrent effect from the incapacitation effect.

Incapacitation and the optimal expected punishment

In the previous chapter, I examined the trade-off between the certainty and severity of punishment in setting the optimal level of expected punishment. When an increase in either the certainty or severity of punishment reduces crime because of the deterrent effect, the authorities can substitute between the two. With respect to prison sentences, this suggests that, to achieve a desired level of expected punishment, as the prison sentence is increased the probability of apprehension and/or conviction can be reduced. But this fundamental trade-off no longer holds if the sole advantage of prison is through the incapacitation effect.

If there is no deterrent effect, determining the optimal length of the prison sentence no longer depends on the level of certainty of punishment. It is still the case that the authorities must choose a desired level of certainty, but the length of the prison sentence only depends on the potential harm a released criminal will inflict upon society. For example, if it is determined that a released criminal will always cause more harm than the cost of incapacitation, the optimal prison sentence is life behind bars. If it is determined that a prisoner, at some point in their life, will cause less harm than the cost of incapacitation, that prisoner can be released. So, for a given level of certainty of punishment, because of the incapacitation effect a lengthy prison sentence or a short prison sentence can be justified *without* concern about continually trading off between the certainty and severity of punishment.

Another important distinction between the deterrent and the incapacitation effects has to do with the relationship between the severity of the prison sentence and the magnitude of the harm caused by the criminal. For optimal deterrence, it is typically the case that the greater the harm caused the more severe the prison sentence. With incapacitation, however, the criminal should remain incarcerated as long as the expected harm from future criminal acts exceeds the cost of incapacitation. This is true if the expected harm just *slightly* exceeds the cost of incapacitation, or *greatly* exceeds the cost.

For example, if a car thief is always expected to impose more costs on society than the cost of incapacitation, that criminal should be incarcerated for life. The same argument will hold true for a murderer, even though murder is likely to be far more harmful than car theft. On the other hand, suppose a man, in a drunken rage, murders someone. If it can be determined that the man will never get drunk again, and is not likely to murder anyone else, the incapacitation costs may exceed the expected future harm. If there is no deterrent effect to prison sentences, in this case it can be argued that the murderer should *not* be imprisoned. Notice, however, that I am not arguing that in the real world murderers should go unpunished. What I am suggesting is that if, hypothetically, the *sole* purpose of prison is to prevent criminals from committing future crimes, to save the resource costs of imprisonment any criminal who is considered unlikely to commit future crimes should not be incapacitated.

With respect to the incapacitation effect, prison can be best thought of as a place for criminals who are most likely to commit *future* crimes. In theory, this suggests that an individual who has yet to commit a crime may need to be incarcerated if an expected future crime is deemed sufficiently harmful. Of course, this would be an extremely difficult policy to implement. To determine who should be incarcerated, it makes sense to identify criminals who have *already* committed harmful acts. Once these criminals are incarcerated, they should be given life sentences until it is determined that they would impose less harm on society than the cost of incapacitation. In a sense, then, the optimal length of a prison sentence would be determined by a prisoner's eligibility for parole.

As can be seen, if there is no deterrent effect, we can make some fairly extreme predictions about how to set the severity of a prison sentence based on the incapacitation effect. From a social policy perspective, this is why it is important to distinguish between the two effects. To determine if there is a deterrent effect of prison, we must look at the available empirical evidence.

The deterrent effect of prison

Before devoting resources to enforce prison sentences, it would be useful to determine that the sanction of prison actually reduces the crime rate. But any empirical study that finds a connection between increased prison sentences and reduced crime rates may not be telling the complete story. It may be important to determine exactly *how* that connection is being made. It doesn't take much imagination to draw a link between reduced crime and the incapacitation effect. To the extent that criminals are likely to be multiple offenders (and there is evidence, presented later, to suggest that this is the case), and that incapacitation actually works (that is, prisoners do not sneak out at night to commit crimes), an incarcerated criminal will not be an active criminal outside of prison. Separating out the deterrent effect from the incapacitation effect, however, is a more difficult task. The trick is to find something in the data that allows researchers to specifically isolate the deterrent effect. Fortunately, there have been several empirical studies that have successfully distinguished between the two effects by examining sentence enhancement laws, juvenile crime, quality of prison life, and the ability of criminals to substitute between different crimes.

Enhanced prison sentences

Sentence enhancement laws abruptly alter prison sentences for specific types of crime. For example, if a current sentence for a violent crime is a ten-year prison sentence, a sentence enhancement law that comes into effect may immediately change that sentence to fifteen years. Due to the nature of how the laws are enacted, it may be possible to separate out the deterrent effect from the incapacitation effect of the increased sentences.

If there is a sudden change in the length of a prison sentence associated with a specific crime, it is likely that, in the short run, the deterrent effect will be more relevant than the incapacitation effect. A criminal who will be facing ten years in prison, and may now be facing fifteen years in prison, will still be facing at least the original ten-year sentence. Thus, any change in the incapacitation effect wouldn't come into play until the start of the additional five-year sentence. This suggests that any immediate change in the crime rate must be due to the deterrent effect of the sentence enhancement. In the long run, however, both the deterrent effect and the incapacitation effect may be reducing the crime rate.

One study (Kessler and Levitt, 1999) examines the effect on crime rates of California's sentence enhancement laws passed in 1982. These particular laws enacted a five-year enhancement for each prior conviction for a serious felony *or* a one-year enhancement for each prior prison term served for any offense, whichever enhancement was greater. Furthermore, the revised laws eliminated the statute of limitations that allowed the courts to consider the defendant's record for at most only the past ten years, prohibited judges from allowing the enhancements to be served concurrently with the base sentence, and required the enhancements themselves to be served consecutively. In all, these were fairly strict enhancements.

Comparing crimes that were eligible for sentence enhancements (murder, rape, robbery, aggravated assault with a firearm, and burglary of a residence) to crimes that were not eligible (aggravated assault without a firearm, burglary of a nonresidence, motor vehicle theft, and larceny), the crime rates for the eligible crimes were found to have dropped in the first year after the enhancements were enacted. Furthermore, there was an even greater drop in the crime rates three years after the law was enacted, and even greater still seven years later. These results suggest that the immediate drop in the crime rates was due to the deterrent effect, but over time the incapacitation effect also kicked in.

From juvenile to adult

It is extremely common when dealing with controversial social issues to distinguish between adults and children. Some activities, while legal for adults to undertake, are illegal for children to undertake. Other activities are illegal for both groups to undertake, yet there are differences between the ways adult offenders and juvenile offenders are dealt with by the authorities. Typically, for an identical crime, a juvenile is likely to be treated more leniently by the justice system than is an adult. There may be good reasons for this distinction but, from a rational crime perspective, the more lenient treatment of juveniles may be leading to increases in juvenile crime.

One study (Levitt, 1998a) examines juvenile crimes for children ages fifteen to seventeen between the years 1978 and 1993. This was a particularly violent period in American history, as violent crime by juveniles and adults dramatically increased (by 107 percent and 52 percent, respectively). During that period, punishment per crime (measured by the number of prisoners per violent crime committed) fell 20 percent for juveniles but increased 60 percent for adults. One of the issues addressed in the study is this: What would have been the increase in the violent crime rate for juveniles *had* they faced the same increase in punishment as did the adults? The answer is that the juvenile violent crime rate would have increased by only 74 percent instead of 107 percent. This result suggests that juvenile criminals are rational in the sense that they do respond to changes in the expected punishment.

Notice that during this period, and with this study's data set, the hypothesized increased punishment for juveniles is leading not to a reduction in the crime rate, but instead to a reduction in the *growth* of the crime rate. Still, this is a meaningful measure of crime reduction. It is possible to examine a period of time and observe that crime rates have increased concurrently with punishment enhancements, and conclude that criminals do not respond to increased punishment. But there are many factors that affect the crime rate. The important point is that the crime rate might have been *higher* if not for the increased punishment.

Demonstrating that juveniles respond to changes in the expected punishment does not directly address the distinction between the deterrent and incapacitation effects of prison. Fortunately, the study is able to separate out these effects for juveniles who reach the age of majority, that is, the age when their classification changes from juvenile to adult. In thirty-seven states and the District of Columbia, the oldest age for juvenile court jurisdiction is seventeen. In ten states, it is sixteen. And in three states (Connecticut, New York, and North Carolina), it is fifteen. In all states, however, exceptions can be made and juvenile offenders below the appropriate age cutoff can still be tried in criminal court and face adult sanctions (Office of Justice Programs/U.S. Department of Justice, *Juvenile Offenders and Victims: 2006 National Report*).

The author finds that in states where adults are punished harshly relative to juveniles, compared to states where the punishment differential is not as severe, there is a substantial drop in the crime rate for the cohort of criminals who have reached the age of majority within the past year. This is a similar idea to the sentence enhancement argument made above. In some states, juveniles reach a point in their lives when all of a sudden they may face a substantial change in the punishment they receive for a particular crime. In the short run, this punishment enhancement can reduce crime through a deterrent effect, as opposed to an incapacitation effect.

The study concludes that increased punishment is an effective deterrence in reducing juvenile crime rates. This result, of course, does not dictate that juveniles and adults should be punished identically. Instead, it simply suggests that increased punishment may be an effective tool. There are likely to be many other considerations to take into account when confronting the social issue of juvenile crime, a topic I return to in Chapter 8.

Quality of prison life

Two prison sentences of equal length have the same ability to reduce crime through the incapacitation effect. But not only does the prison sentence in and of itself reduce the crime rate, in addition the *quality* of prison life may be a factor. For example, for a specific sentence length, a very harsh prison environment is likely to have a stronger deterrent effect than would a less harsh environment.

There are many factors that affect the quality of life in prison. What are the living conditions? Is there excessive prisoner congestion? Are there activities available such as exercise equipment, cable television, library access, job training, education, and so on? Is there prisoner violence against each other? And the list can go on. Despite the existence of all of these factors, to undertake an empirical study to measure the deterrent effect of the quality of prison life there must be some *available* data.

One study (Katz, Levitt and Shustorovich, 2003) uses the death rate from *all* causes (except executions) among prisoners as a proxy for the quality of prison life: the higher the death rate, the lower the quality of prison life. Throughout the sample period of 1950 to 1990, the average number of annual prison deaths per 1,000 prisoners was 3.10. Although a further disaggregation of causes of death were not available for the sample period, the authors use data for the representative year of 1997 to show that approximately 77 percent of prison deaths were due to illness, 5 percent to suicides, 3 percent to accidents or killing by another inmate, and 12 percent to unspecified causes (and 2 percent due to executions).

Prisoner death rate is far from a perfect measure of the quality of prison life. To the extent that prisoners die of natural causes, that may have little to do with an adverse quality of prison life. Instead, it is likely that the prisoner death rate is *correlated* with several unpleasant aspects of prison life, such as inadequate health care, suicide, and homicide. As long as the death rate is a reasonable proxy for the quality of prison life, even if it is not a perfect proxy, it may be used to measure the effect of prison life on the crime rate.

The main result of the study is that there is a negative relationship between the prison death rate and the crime rate. This holds true for both violent crime and property crime. If the prison death rate is a reasonable proxy for the quality of prison life, as that quality is lowered the crime rate is also lowered. This result may suggest that an important policy tool in deterring crime may be to purposely eliminate activities from prison that improve the quality of life for prisoners. But, as the authors point out, there are going to be several other social concerns about the quality of prison life that may be as important as, or more important than, the deterrence aspect.

With regard to these other social concerns, there are human rights organizations that monitor prison conditions throughout the world and publicize poor or abusive treatment of prisoners. One such group, Human Rights Watch, lists many examples of poor prison conditions on its website (hrw.org). Such examples include: twenty-five inmates killed in Modelo prison in Bogotà (Colombia) during a riot in April, 2000; approximately 10 percent of Russian prisoners are infected with tuberculosis; in some Brazilian police lockups, overcrowding is so acute that some prisoners have to tie themselves to the cell bars to sleep; in Haiti, women prisoners are often held with male prisoners, exposing the women to sexual abuse and violence; and there are many incidents of physical abuse and extortion of prisoners by guards. While these poor conditions may create an enhanced deterrent effect, they also raise troubling questions about the appropriate social goals of a prison system.

Crime substitutes

One interesting study (Levitt, 1998b) attempts to distinguish between, and measure the relative importance of, the deterrent and incapacitation effects by building on three key assumptions. First, the typical criminal must be a multiple offender. If the typical criminal is likely to commit only one crime in their lifetime, the incapacitation effect would not reduce the crime rate unless the criminal could be imprisoned *before* the crime is committed. Thus, any study attempting to measure the incapacitation effect must be looking at criminals who are or would be (if not imprisoned) multiple offenders. Second, the typical criminal must be likely to commit different types of crime. For example, a particular criminal may not only be a car thief, but may also enjoy committing the occasional burglary.

These first two assumptions appear to be well supported by real-world evidence. The author cites evidence based on prisoner surveys that the average number of (nondrug-related) crimes committed in the year preceding an inmate's most recent arrest is between twelve and fifteen. That is certainly an indication of multiple offense behavior. As for committing different types of crimes, evidence indicates that many criminals do not specialize in one type of crime. For example, only one in twenty released murderers who commit crimes post-release will have their next arrest be for murder. For released robbers and automobile thieves the corresponding number is approximately one in three. And for burglars and larcenists the number is approximately one in two.

As for the third assumption, there must be some crimes that are *substitutes* for each other. What this explicitly means is that, if the expected punishment is increased for one particular crime only, a criminal will substitute away from committing that crime and instead commit another crime. It is the existence of substitute crimes that allows a distinction between the deterrent and incapacitation effects.

With deterrence, an increase in the expected punishment of one crime will reduce the occurrence of that crime, but *increase* the occurrence of a substitute crime.

For example, if the expected punishment for car theft is increased while the expected punishment for burglary is kept the same, a car thief may decide to switch to burglary. With incapacitation, an increase in the expected punishment of one crime will reduce the occurrence of that crime, but also will *reduce* the occurrence of a substitute crime because imprisonment prevents the criminal from committing further crimes.

The author empirically examines seven crime categories to determine the extent of the deterrent and incapacitation effects. With the data used in this particular study, for the least severe but by far the most common crimes (accounting for 90 percent of all crimes) – aggravated assault, burglary, larceny, and auto theft – the deterrent effect appears to be more important than the incapacitation effect. For rape and robbery, the opposite is true. Finally, for murder, neither effect appears to be particularly important. The study concludes, along with the others discussed above, that the deterrent effect does exist and can be distinguished from the incapacitation effect.

The inequality of equal prison sentences

A popularly held criticism of the criminal justice system is that wealthy defendants and poor defendants are not treated equally. If wealthy (relative to poor) defendants are able to hire more expensive and, therefore, more effective legal representation, they may face lower conviction rates for similar crimes. In other words, it is often argued that wealthy defendants are able to *subvert* justice. Instead of examining the accuracy of this criticism, I am going to accept as *fact* that wealthy and poor defendants are treated differently by the criminal justice system and use economic analysis to raise what may appear to be an unusual question: Is it *efficient* for a wealthy defendant to face a lower probability of conviction?

If we assume that prison sentences are largely determined by the nature of the crime (as opposed to the wealth of the criminal), a poor defendant and a wealthy defendant may face the same prison sentence for the same crime if convicted. But if the wealthy defendant can effectively lower the probability of conviction, that defendant faces a lower *expected* punishment than does the poor defendant. This implies that, compared to a poor defendant, a wealthy defendant is more likely to go unpunished. If this difference in expected punishments between the wealthy and poor is deemed to be a social problem, there are ways to remedy it.

First, constraints may be imposed on how much a wealthy defendant can spend on a legal defense, thus possibly increasing the probability of conviction. Defense attorneys are unlikely to be excited about this reform. Second, if the wealthy are permitted to spend at will on their defense, they can be sentenced to longer prison sentences than the poor will face, thus balancing out the lower certainty of punishment with a higher severity of punishment. Finally, more resources can be provided to the poor so that they can mount stronger defenses, thus lowering their probability of conviction. While the first two reforms are unlikely ever to be seriously considered, there is often discussion of reform in providing legal services to poor defendants.

For example, in 2001 the Texas State Bar Board of Directors issued a document entitled *Standards for the Provisions of Legal Services to the Poor in Criminal Matters*. In this document, eight objectives are stated:

> A system for providing legal services to the poor in criminal matters should guarantee that quality legal representation is afforded to all person eligible for counsel.
>
> Each jurisdiction shall have a plan by which effective legal representation is provided in a timely manner to those eligible for such representation.
>
> Any plan for providing legal representation in each jurisdiction shall be designed to ensure that counsel assigned to represent indigent clients have the appropriate qualifications and experience to handle the legal matters assigned to them.
>
> The system for providing legal representation in each jurisdiction shall be designed to guarantee the integrity of the relationship between lawyer and client. The plan and lawyers serving under it should be free from judicial and political influence and should be subject to judicial supervision only in the same manner and to the same extent as are prosecutors.
>
> The system for providing legal representation shall provide for investigatory, expert, and other services necessary and sufficient to an effective defense. These should include not only those services and facilities needed for an effective defense at trial, but also those that are required for effective defense participation in every phase of the process.
>
> Counsel designated to provide legal representation to those eligible shall be compensated for time and service performed in accordance with prevailing standards.
>
> Government entities have the responsibility to provide adequate funding for legal representation for all eligible persons. In particular, the state has a duty to guarantee adequate funding so that the prosecution and sentencing decisions are not dictated by the financial resources of the county. Under no circumstances should the funding power interfere with or retaliate against professional judgments made in the proper discharge of defense services.
>
> The legal representation plan shall have in place machinery to monitor the quality of legal representation provided to indigent clients.

These objectives clearly demonstrate the willingness of the authorities to address the issue of providing the poor with adequate legal representation, possibly to level the playing field between poor and wealthy defendants. Critics, however, point out that resources used by the wealthy are *private*, while resources used by the state are *public*. This creates an additional burden of being concerned about how best to use public resources in pursuing criminal justice social goals.

All of the above suggestions are attempting to achieve the goal of maintaining equal expected punishments for wealthy and poor defendants facing the same criminal charges. But if a wealthy defendant and a poor one face the same certainty of receiving the same prison sentence, it can be argued that the wealthy defendant is being punished *more* harshly. The key to this seemingly strange argument involves the concept of *opportunity cost*.

An opportunity cost takes into account a forgone alternative. For example, your opportunity cost of currently reading this book is what you would be doing instead. Would you be sleeping, eating, watching a movie, or reading another book? Whatever is your best forgone alternative, that makes up part of the cost of your reading this book. As another example, university students not only incur the tuition costs and room and board fees of being in school, they incur an opportunity cost in terms of their best forgone alternative, which most likely would be some kind of employment. Even if an activity does not have a direct monetary cost, its opportunity cost is an important concept to consider.

There is no doubt that prisoners face substantial opportunity costs. Of primary importance for this discussion is the loss in legitimate income. The more income a prisoner could be making if *not* imprisoned, the higher the opportunity cost of being imprisoned. To accept the argument that an equal prison sentence for a wealthy and poor defendant is harsher for the wealthy one, one must accept the contention that a wealthy defendant has a higher opportunity cost of being imprisoned relative to a poor defendant. If we consider only lost income opportunities, this may be a valid way to think. But there may be other opportunity costs of being imprisoned, such as lost time with family and friends, or not being able to enjoy certain leisure activities. Thus, I am not claiming that poor prisoners face no opportunity costs of being imprisoned, and many may even face very high opportunity costs. But to the extent that lost income is an important component of the opportunity cost of prison, a wealthy defendant is likely to face a higher opportunity cost than does a poor defendant.

If it is optimal for a particular crime to warrant a particular expected punishment, *and* if the opportunity cost of a specific prison sentence is higher for a wealthy defendant relative to a poor defendant, the probability of conviction must be set lower for the wealthy defendant. If not, and the probability of conviction is the same for each defendant, an identical prison sentence for all defendants cannot lead to an optimal expected punishment for everyone.

For example, if a prison sentence is set just long enough to optimally punish very wealthy defendants, poorer defendants will be *under*deterred because of the short sentence. If the sentence is set long enough to optimally punish poor defendants, wealthier defendants will be *over*deterred because of their relatively high opportunity costs. And if the sentence is set to optimally punish the average defendant, wealthier defendants will be overdeterred *and* poorer defendants will be underdeterred. Thus, allowing a wealthy defendant to "subvert" the justice system may actually be leading to equal expected punishments across wealth classes.

Alternatively, it may seem reasonable to devote fewer resources to imprisoning criminals by lowering the sentences of wealthy defendants, but this may be difficult to do correctly. Opportunity costs can be highly subjective in nature, so it may be difficult for the authorities to correctly differentiate prison sentences based on a criminal's opportunity cost. If all criminals face the same prison sentence for the same crime, the criminals themselves can decide how many resources to devote to their defense to try to reduce the probability of conviction. It is important to note, however, that while wealthy defendants may try to lower their probability of conviction, prosecutors may counter by increasing the amount of resources they use in trying wealthy defendants. But how well can prosecutors stretch their resources to combat wealthy defendants?

It may appear that a sensible prosecutorial goal would be to try to equate the probability of conviction across different types of defendants charged with committing a particular crime. This suggests that more resources should be devoted to defendants who mount more expensive defenses. But there may be some problems with this approach. First, wealthy defendants may have far more flexibility in their spending than will prosecutors. If a prosecutorial budget can only be stretched so far, wealthy defendants may be able to successfully outspend the prosecutors, thus leading to lower conviction rates for the wealthy relative to the poor. Second, even if prosecutors can match wealthy defendants, there is the issue as to whether or not the additional resources can be put to more efficient use in other aspects of setting the expected punishment, such as with increasing the probability of apprehension. Finally, if too many resources are moved from prosecuting poor defendants to prosecuting wealthy defendants, the poor defendants may face too low a probability of conviction. This implies that poor defendants may be underdeterred. Actually, some scholars believe that the existence of wealthy defendants in and of itself *benefits* poorer defendants because of this last point.

In all, it is unlikely that wealthy defendants with high opportunity costs will be able to successfully lower conviction rates to make equal prison sentences yield equal expected punishment. It is more likely that, for whatever prison sentence is set for a particular crime, the wealthiest defendants will be overdeterred, and the poorest defendants will be underdeterred. Still, the ability of wealthy defendants to "subvert" justice to any extent may actually be leading to more efficient levels of expected punishment.

It is important to note that the argument being made in this section is not that the wealthy should be less severely punished than the poor. The argument is that if it is desirable to maintain an equal level of expected punishment for an identical crime, equal conviction rates and equal prison sentences for the wealthy and poor may not achieve that goal. If prison imposes more of a cost on a wealthy criminal, a lower conviction rate is necessary to maintain a consistent expected punishment across income groups. In effect, expected punishment can be a broader concept than what is determined by the authorities when they set the certainty and severity of punishment. Different defendants can perceive identical sanctions to have different subjective impacts on their behavior.

The privatization of prisons

A common issue in many social policy debates is the role of private versus social control of resources. Are private markets or socialized systems better suited to provide health care, offer schooling, build highways, and so on? The succinct argument in favor of privatization is that, relative to social systems, private firms use resources more efficiently in the provision of services. The goal of a private firm is to maximize profit, which requires (for any given level of services) cost minimization. A private firm makes investment decisions typically based solely on the dollar bottom line, whereas, in a social system, politicians may have additional political objectives. Policy makers do not directly bear the costs of their actions; taxpayers do. Cost minimization, then, may not be of primary importance in social systems.

On the other hand, a common criticism of privatization is that a private firm may cut corners and provide poor-quality services in order to enhance their profit margin. And, even in the case where private firms do not or cannot slack, there may be other legitimate social objectives that a private firm would ignore to the possible detriment of social welfare. For example, is it a sound social goal to provide education to all children, even to those whose parents could not afford to send them to private schools? Should health care be available to all, or only to those who can afford the services or the insurance premiums? Exactly what constitutes "good" educational or health care services? There are no easy answers to these questions, especially due to the fact that the answers rely on subjective policy goals. Nevertheless, these are important social policy issues.

Even if there is a wedge between private and social objectives, this does not rule out the possibility of the state enlisting private companies to further social goals. What is needed to provide the private companies with the appropriate social objectives, however, are well specified contracts that lay out the ground rules of operation. With well specified contracts, the state may have the opportunity to take advantage of the potential cost efficiencies a private company can provide, as well as sustain any other objectives that are less likely to be in the interest of private operators. But two substantial hurdles remain: it may be difficult, if not impossible, to negotiate fully specified contracts; and, even with fully specified contracts, it may be difficult to enforce the contractual terms.

The running of prisons offers an excellent illustration of the potential tensions between private and social interests. Private prisons are fairly common, and becoming more common, in the United States. In 2000, of the 1,668 adult correctional facilities, 84 were federal, 1,320 were state, and 264 were private-run operations. Federal institutions had a rated capacity for 83,000 inmates, state institutions for 1.1 million inmates, and private institutions for 105,000 inmates. Just five years earlier, there were only 110 private prisons with a rated capacity of 19,000 inmates (Bureau of Justice Statistics, *Census of State and Federal Correctional Facilities, 2000*).

In theory, the services associated with prison can easily be provided through private or public ownership. These services can be divided into three main categories – order, amenities, and rehabilitation. Order includes such services as security, preventing escapes, and disciplining prisoners. Amenities include food preparation, health care, libraries, and entertainment activities. Rehabilitation includes vocational training and other educational activities. The quality of many of these services can be defined by best-practice standards issued by the American

Correctional Association (ACA). Prisons wishing to maintain accreditation must adhere to a majority of over 400 of the ACA standards. Thus, if the state wishes to contract with private prisons, contracts can be specified such that the prisons can be held to well publicized and well defined standards. And, for many of the services, contracting does appear to provide the necessary incentives for private prisons to maintain appropriate standards.

Furthermore, there does appear to be evidence of cost savings associated with private prisons. In Colorado, for example, in June, 2006, one in five inmates was housed in a private prison. The annual cost per inmate in a privately operated prison was $18,947. The annual rate per inmate in a state-operated prison was $24,722. The projection for 2008 is that one in three Colorado inmates will be housed in private prisons (*Colorado Springs Gazette*, July 31, 2006). Cost savings, however, are only part of the issue.

For some prison services, contracting may be insufficient. Two areas of concern in terms of the private provision of prison services involve the use of force and the quality of personnel. Obviously, controlling a population of prisoners will often times require force. How much force in any given situation is warranted? Applying general standards to what will usually be specific episodes of prisoner misconduct may be difficult to do. Furthermore, if private prisons save on costs by hiring less able guards, or by providing poorer training opportunities, prison personnel may simply lack the skill to resolve conflicts with more subtle methods that don't over-rely on the use of force. If contracting cannot adequately guarantee that a private prison will hire the appropriate quality personnel, or have their personnel act within acceptable boundaries, the case for privatization is weakened. This reasoning may help account for the fact that private prisons are most often used for minimum security, juvenile corrections, and halfway houses. Of the 264 private prisons in 2000, four were maximum security, sixty-five were medium security, and 195 were minimum or low security (Bureau of Justice Statistics, *Census of State and Federal Correctional Facilities, 2000*). Maximum security institutions are typically under the control of state or federal authorities.

While private prisons may have a serious down side in terms of quality of services provided, from an economic perspective they are generally thought of as providing these services by using resources efficiently. It is hard to imagine economists criticizing private prisons for being *too* cost-efficient, yet there is an unusual argument against privatization for precisely this reason. In Chapter 2 I argued that there are problems with using low-cost punishments, such as fines or forfeiture of property, because self-interested authorities may have the incentive to overdeter crime for personal financial gain. But what about a very low probability sanction that is physically harsh, such as flogging? Unless the authorities are sadists, there is no personal gain that can be achieved from flogging criminals. If flogging is relatively less expensive to impose than prison sentences, why do we not commonly observe these harsh punishments?

Perhaps the simplest explanation for why harsh sanctions are not used is that society doesn't have a taste for such forms of punishment. This may account for why there is a constitutional protection against cruel and unusual punishment. But for any type of punishment of a brutal nature, we can always find a probability of certainty that makes the expected punishment equal to any other expected punishment with a less severe sanction. Maybe a slight chance of being flogged is equivalent to a larger chance of being imprisoned for a number of years. In other words, does "cruel and unusual" refer only to the nature of the sanction, or does it take into account the *expected* punishment? And if two sanctions, one harsher than the other, can lead to the same expected punishment, yet the harsher punishment uses far fewer resources, is it still necessarily the case that society would have a taste for the more costly, less severe, punishment? These types of questions have led some economists to expand their thinking to offer explanations as to why seemingly inefficient punishments, such as costly prison sentences, may be efficient after all.

Even if there is no personal financial gain from punishing criminals, there may be other types of gain. Elected officials, for example, may be concerned with their personal views on crime and punishment, or the views of their non-criminal electorate. Criminals, however, are also part of society. As I have previously discussed, many rational crime models, when discussing the optimal crime rate, take into account the benefits criminals receive from committing crimes. Exactly how to include criminals into a social welfare analysis is an open question, but if elected officials place little or no weight on criminals, there may be a tendency to overpunish them. In other words, with harsh, low-cost sanctions, elected officials may consider deviating from some social concept of optimal punishment, primarily because it is not costly to deviate. But if a sanction is costly to use, such as prison, the elected officials will be constrained as to how much punishment they can inflict on criminals, and this may enhance social welfare.

Furthermore, some argue that, if private prisons are cost-efficient, too many of them may be built. But what is meant by "too many" prisons? For example, as I will discuss in Chapter 7, much prison space is occupied by criminals involved in some aspect of illicit drug dealing. There are many who feel that drugs should be decriminalized, or at least that drug users should not be heavily punished. If private prisons are relatively cheap to build and maintain, and it is politically expedient to imprison drug users, then from this perspective too many prisons may be built. Thus, a high resource cost punishment such as publicly maintained prisons may be an efficient form of punishment, especially when considering more complicated objectives the authorities may have.

In all, while prison is a costly sanction for the authorities to implement, there do appear to be significant offsetting benefits in terms of both the deterrent and incapacitation effects reducing the crime rate. There may be controversial issues associated with how best to build and maintain prisons, but a prison sentence is widely considered a reasonable form of punishment. Now that I have considered two of the most common sanctions – fines and prison – the next chapter discusses the costs and benefits of the death penalty, currently a legally accepted sanction in the United States, but by far the most controversial punishment of the three.

Notes

Papers distinguishing between the incapacitation and deterrent effects of prison are by Shavell (1987b), Levitt (1998a, 1998b), Kessler and Levitt (1999), and Katz, Levitt, and Shustorovich (2003). On a related topic, papers on the deterrent effect of sentence enhancement through the "three strikes" laws are by Marvell and Moody (2001) and Shepherd (2002).

Other papers on various aspects of prison are by Levitt (1996) on prison overcrowding, Polinsky and Shavell (1999) on inmates discounting the future and the impact on the deterrent effect of sentence length, and Listokin (2003) on the simultaneity of incarceration rates and crime rates. Avio (2000) provides a nice survey of the economics of prisons.

Papers on wealthy versus poor defendants and the concept of justice are by Lott (1987), Kobayashi and Lott (1996), Farmer and Terrell (2001), Goodman and Porter (2002), and Garoupa and Gravelle (2003).

Papers on the costs and benefits of private versus public prisons are by Domberger and Jensen (1997), Hart, Shleifer, and Vishny (1997), Friedman (1999), Benson (2003), Wickelgren (2003), and Bayer and Pozen (2005).

4 The death penalty and crime deterrence

By year end 2005, a total of 3,254 inmates were under sentence of death in the United States. California had the largest number of Death Row inmates, with 646, followed by Texas (411) and Florida (372). Of the 3,254 inmates, 1,805 were white, 1,372 were black, thirty-one were American Indian, thirty-four were Asian, and twelve were of unknown race. In addition, 362 of the inmates were Hispanic (who are at times, depending on the data set, classified as white or black), and fifty-two were women. In 2005, sixty executions occurred, nineteen in Texas, with the next highest number being five in several other states. Of the executed inmates, fifty-nine were men, thirty-eight were white, nineteen black, and three Hispanic (all white). All of the executions were carried out by lethal injection. Only twelve states and the District of Columbia were without the death penalty at that time (Bureau of Justice Statistics, *Capital Punishment, 2005*).

The United States is not the only country that struggles with the controversial death penalty issue. As of February, 2006, there were 109 Death Row convicts in Taiwan. Although there is a political movement to abolish the death penalty there, three of the seventeen inmates sentenced to death in 2005 had been executed by early 2006 (*Taipei Times*, February 20, 2006.) In Australia, a nation that has opposed the death penalty for over forty years (the last execution was in 1967), Prime Minister John Howard went on record as saying that the death penalty would be an appropriate punishment for terrorists, such as those who killed 202 people (eighty-eight of them Australians) in the Bali bombing in 2002 (CNSNews.com, August 20, 2003). After the killing of a police officer in Bradford, U.K., in 2005, ex-Metropolitan Police chief Lord Stevens called for the reinstatement of the death penalty in Britain for people who kill police (BBC News, November 21, 2005). Many other countries, such as Mexico, Canada, members of the European Union, New Zealand, and so on, currently debate the role of the death penalty in their respective criminal justice systems.

If you've ever wondered why economics is sometimes referred to as the dismal science, a thorough reading of the economic research on the deterrent effect of the death penalty may help explain it. Consider the following conclusions from two death penalty studies:

> Recent empirical studies have shown, without exception, that capital punishment deters crime. Using large data sets that combine information from all fifty states over many years, the studies show that, on average, an additional execution deters many murders.
>
> (Joanna Shepherd, Ph.D. economics, *Michigan Law Review,* 2005)

> The U.S. data simply do not speak clearly about whether the death penalty has a deterrent or anti-deterrent effect. The only clear conclusion is that execution policy drives little of the year-to-year variation in homicide rates. As to whether executions raise or lower the homicide rate, we remain profoundly uncertain.
>
> (John J. Donohue III and Justin Wolfers, both Ph.D. economics,
> *Stanford Law Review,* 2005)

Not only do different studies reach opposing conclusions, sometimes a single study can yield mixed results. And these controversial studies are not just used for academic purposes – they enter into the public debate about the death penalty. I have heard experts on television news shows claim that there is incontrovertible evidence demonstrating that the death penalty deters murder. In my opinion, that claim is an overstatement. I have also heard experts claim that there is no evidence that the death penalty deters murder. That claim is simply incorrect.

When it comes to choosing sides in the debate over the ability of the death penalty to deter murder, I believe there are two equally credible statements that can be made:

> There is a substantial amount of empirical evidence to support the claim that the death penalty deters murder.
> There is a substantial amount of empirical evidence that does not support the claim that the death penalty deters murder.

If you think that I am painting economics in a bad light, I'm really not. The inconsistencies in the results of empirical studies concerning the death penalty have little to do with the way economists use economic reasoning to address the issue. In fact, there is a strong consensus among economists concerning the *theoretical* underpinning of the ability of the death penalty to deter murder. That underpinning relies on the assumption of rational criminal behavior.

With rational criminals, if the death penalty is a harsher punishment than life imprisonment, this increase in the severity of punishment is predicted to reduce the crime rate. I believe most economists accept this basic premise, at least as a starting point, despite whatever skepticism may exist among other scholars or laymen over the assumption of rational criminal behavior. But, as I have discussed previously, it is not all criminals who must behave rationally for harsher punishment to deter crime. Even when considering rational criminal behavior, there may be several reasons why the death penalty does not have a deterrent effect. So even if all economists agree on the use of economic reasoning to raise the question of a deterrent effect, that question ultimately must be answered empirically. And by the nature of empirical work, especially in the social sciences, a definitive answer may never be found.

Does the deterrent effect exist?

While the many empirical studies on the deterrent effect of the death penalty differ in important ways, at their core there is a much in common. A typical approach is to estimate the deterrent effect by comparing murder rates across states that enforce the death penalty versus states that do not enforce it. Another approach is to focus more on intrastate murder rates for states that have changed their policy stance over time: Does the murder rate increase after a moratorium is imposed, and does the murder rate decrease after a moratorium is lifted? Also, it is possible to compare execution *rates* and their effect on murder rates across states that enforce the death penalty. What is most important in economic studies, however, is the inclusion of control variables to isolate the potential deterrent effect of the death penalty.

With death penalty studies, as is always the case with empirical work, there is a wide variety of control variables that are used, but most studies include the three main categories discussed in Chapter 1: *deterrent* variables, such as the probabilities of apprehension and conviction; *economic* variables, such as per capita income and the unemployment rate; and, *demographic* variables, such as population density, gender, age, and race. These types of controls are crucial to consider. For example, if a state that enforces the death penalty appears to have a lower murder rate than a state that does not enforce it, it is important to make sure that the lower murder rate cannot be attributed to some other factor such as a higher probability of apprehension, or a lower unemployment rate, or a smaller population density. Even though not all other factors can be controlled, either because they can't all be identified or, more commonly, adequate data do not exist, the more relevant variables that can be controlled the more reliable the results.

For studies that conclude that the death penalty does lead to a statistically significant deterrent effect, the result is often expressed in terms of number of murders deterred (that is, number of lives saved) for each convicted criminal that is actually executed. This is often referred to as a *life–life trade-off*. For example, one study (Dezhbakhsh, Rubin, and Shepherd, 2003) finds that on average, each execution deters eighteen murders. There are many other studies that reach a similar conclusion, even though the quantitative measurement of the life–life trade-off does vary substantially. In short, there is a body of literature that offers empirical verification of the deterrent effect of the death penalty. Those who claim that there is no such evidence, are mistaken. On the other hand, for those who claim that the evidence is unreliable, that is another matter entirely.

A common approach to casting doubt on the empirical verification of the deterrent effect of the death penalty is to attempt to replicate the result of the original studies, and then put the data through the ringer by doing a battery of robustness tests. It is common that the deterrent effect result does not seem to stand up well to these robustness tests. Small changes in the empirical specifications often lead to a finding of a statistically insignificant deterrent effect or, even worse, the perverse result that each execution leads to an *increase* in the murder rate (the so-called *brutalization effect*).

A study by two authors (Donohue and Wolfers, 2005) offers an excellent example of how difficult it is to place much confidence in the empirical verification of the deterrent effect. The authors have access to much of the data used in previous studies, and replicate numerous approaches to verifying the deterrent effect of the death penalty. They find that *none* of the approaches stands up well to robustness tests, and conclude that the evidence does not confirm that the death penalty affects the murder rate. And while both sides continue to argue the issue passionately, at least it is encouraging that there is much data-sharing in this literature. To the extent that researchers share their data so that replication and specification tests are more easily accomplished, more confidence can be placed in the fact that, for many of the authors of these studies, it is the ultimate empirical "truth" that is being sought, and not just some personal agenda that is being advanced.

But even if a personal agenda is not being sought, sincere researcher bias can still affect the results of a study. One author (Leamer, 1983) uses death penalty data to explore this point. To determine if there is a deterrent effect of capital punishment, the author examines cross-state variation in the murder rate (defined as murders per 100,000 population), and uses the three standard groups of control variables: deterrent variables (probability of conviction, probability of execution, average prison time served by murderers); economic variables (average family income, poverty rate, unemployment rate); and, demographic variables (percent nonwhite, percent fifteen to twenty-four years old, percent male, percent two-parent families), and a few other variables that fit into one of the above categories.

First, the author estimates a regression equation using *all* of the control variables and finds that, on average, each additional execution deters thirteen murders. But how well does this result hold up if different combinations of the control variables are used? Furthermore, what combination of the control variables are *appropriate* to use? This is where researcher bias comes into play, and this is the author's main concern.

Researcher bias need not be insincere. Certainly, there may be researchers who have a preconceived result in mind and manipulate the data until that result is confirmed – "I believe in the deterrent effect and I'm going to find it!" But researcher bias may also be sincere in that there is a belief that, from a theoretical perspective, certain control variables are more relevant than others.

For example, one group of researchers (the author labels as "right-wingers") may believe that the deterrent variables are important in explaining the murder rate, but doubt the relevance of the economic and demographic variables. By estimating numerous regressions that include the deterrent variables and other possible combinations of the other variables, these researchers always find a positive deterrent effect (ranging from a high of 22.56 to a low of 0.86 lives saved for each execution). In other words, the "right-winger" believes that the deterrent variables *must* be included, and, as long as they are, a deterrent effect is found to exist and is strongly robust to many other possible regression specifications. This is a very strong result, and suggests that the researcher is avoiding any claim of bias because of the numerous regressions that are examined.

But now consider another group of researchers (the author labels as "bleeding hearts"). This group believes that economic variables are important in explaining the murder rate, but doubt the relevance of the deterrent and demographic variables. By estimating many regressions that include the economic variables and other possible combinations of the other variables, these researchers find that a deterrent effect may or may not exist (ranging from 25.59 lives saved to 12.37 lives *lost* for each execution).

Each group of researchers believe they have strong results and are avoiding any claim of bias because they are examining numerous regression specifications. They simply differ as to which variables *necessarily* matter, and which variables may or may not matter. After considering three other possible groups of researchers, the significance of the deterrent variables is seen to strongly depend on the specifications used, and the author concludes that "any inference from these data about the deterrent effect of capital punishment is too fragile to be believed" (Leamer, 1983, p. 42).

Perhaps it isn't surprising that the empirical verification of the deterrent effect does not stand up well to robustness tests. The data used in these studies are fairly thin. In the United States between the years 1930 and 2005 there were a total of 4,863 executions, and between the years 1968 and 1976, due to a national moratorium, there was none. After the moratorium was lifted, between the years 1977 and 2005 there were over a half-million homicides, but only 1,004 executions (Bureau of Justice Statistics, *Capital Punishment*, 2005; *Homicide Trends in the United States*, 2005). Thus, the sentence of capital punishment has not often been applied in murder cases, and, even when applied, it has not been strongly enforced. Interestingly, one of the great ironies of the economic studies that demonstrate the existence of a deterrent effect of the death penalty is that they may be inadvertently *refuting* the concept of rational criminal behavior.

It appears to be an empirical fact that the probability of being executed conditional on committing murder is very small (approximately one in 200, depending on the data used, see Levitt, 2004). Furthermore, even if sentenced to death, there is a long lag between sentencing and execution. Taken together, what criminal is likely to be deterred by a punishment that is very unlikely to be carried out and, even then, not until well into the future? The *irrational* criminal who grossly overestimates the impact of the deterrent effect. Thus, it may very well be the case that a rational criminal has little to fear from the death penalty.

But one must be cautious in arguing against the death penalty simply because its deterrent effect is difficult to verify empirically. The shortcoming with the death penalty may be due not to the death penalty in and of itself, but instead to the way in which the sentence is implemented in the real world. Perhaps a more certain and quicker implementation of the death penalty would yield a verifiable deterrent effect. In fact, there is a small amount of empirical evidence to support that claim. One study (Shepherd, 2004) finds that, on average, one extra murder is deterred for every 2.75 year reduction in a convict's wait on death row before execution takes place. Another study (Shepherd, 2005) finds that, on average, if a state performs nine executions during the twenty-year sample period (1977–96), there are enough executions to create a deterrent effect. With fewer than nine executions, a state that enforces the death penalty either does not generate a deterrent effect, or there is evidence of a brutalization effect. Of course, the robustness of these results is always in question, but the intuition behind the results is sound – change the way the death penalty is implemented and its potential deterrent effect may be more apparent.

One other study on the death penalty (Ekelund, Jackson, Ressler and Tollison, 2006) finds that while a deterrent effect exists for single murders, the effect does not exist for *multiple* murders. The reasoning behind this result is straightforward. If a criminal faces the death penalty for a first murder, additional murders cannot increase the severity of punishment. From a cost–benefit perspective, then, the rational criminal does not consider facing harsher punishment for further murders. The authors suggest that, to dissuade criminals from committing multiple murders, some gradation of severity of punishment should be considered. One interesting gradation involves the *form* of execution that is used. The authors find that a harsh form of execution, such as electrocution, imposes a stronger deterrent effect on single murders than does a less harsh form such as lethal injection. If this is true, it is possible to punish successive murders with different forms of execution – lethal injection for a single murder, the gas chamber for two murders, the electric chair for three, and so on. It is also possible to punish multiple murderers with a mixture of costly prison time, such as hard labor for a number of years, and *then* impose the death penalty. It is also possible to mix substantial fines with prison and execution based on the number of murders committed. Of course, the authorities can also manipulate the certainty of punishment to impose different expected punishments on single versus multiple murderers. As the Old West bank robbers had to consider, if serial killers face higher probabilities of apprehension and conviction than do single murderers, both types can face the same severity of punishment yet different expected punishments.

In all, the debate over the death penalty among economists is centered around whether there is a way to demonstrate that a deterrent effect exists. As of now, it appears that this issue remains unresolved, largely due to the eccentricities of empirical research. Still, in terms of social policy, the deterrent effect is considered to be of utmost importance to the analysis, primarily because it is thought of as the greatest benefit associated with the death penalty. But what does economic reasoning have to say about the greatest cost of using the death penalty – the possibility of an innocent person being wrongfully executed?

Wrongful conviction and the death penalty

No matter on which side of the death penalty debate you currently find yourself, there is no denying the fact that the possibility of an innocent defendant being wrongfully convicted and executed is abhorrent. One can argue that there are already several built-in mechanisms to protect the rights of a defendant, and that the legal system is designed to allow for a large number of wrongful acquittals in place of a single wrongful conviction. Actually, there is even a well publicized ratio of 10:1 (known as the "Blackstone ratio") of acceptable wrongful acquittals relative to wrongful convictions. But as long as convictions occur, there undoubtedly will be incorrect ones. Thus, wrongful convictions are an integral part of the criminal justice system, regardless of what punishment convicted defendants face, but an interesting question remains: Does the probability of a wrongful conviction *depend* on the severity of the punishment?

Consider the facts of the following criminal case, largely based on real-world events. An eighteen-year-old man was accused of raping a fifteen-year-old girl. During the trial, it was made clear that the two did have a sexual relationship, but whether it was consensual was at issue. The jury ending up believing that it was consensual, and so acquitted the young man of rape charges. However, the crime of having sex with a minor was proven beyond a reasonable doubt, and the jury found him guilty of statutory rape. At sentencing, the judge relied on a rarely used law that allowed the defendant to be sentenced to ten years in prison without the possibility of parole. Upon hearing of the sentence, many of the jurors claimed that, had they known how harsh the sentence was going to be, they would have acquitted the man of statutory rape charges. In other words, the degree of the punishment itself would have lowered the probability of conviction.

Although the above example does not involve the death penalty, the intuition is the same. If jurors must find a defendant guilty beyond a *reasonable doubt*, the evidence that is presented must be perceived by each juror to be beyond that threshold. It is possible that the reasonable doubt threshold is perceived to be dependent on the degree of punishment. For example, in a death penalty case, a juror may hold the prosecution to a higher degree of evidence to prove reasonable doubt than would be the case if the ultimate punishment was life imprisonment. If sanctions are perceived as being too harsh for a particular crime, a jury may be more demanding before they vote to convict. This implies that the harsher a sentence is for a given crime the lower will be the probability of conviction, which means there will be fewer correct *and* fewer wrongful convictions.

It may be quite difficult to design social policy to reduce wrongful convictions without also increasing wrongful acquittals. In general, to reduce the number of wrongful convictions, you must reduce the number of convictions, thus reducing both wrongful and correct convictions. For example, if the rules of evidence are changed in the defendant's favor and it becomes more difficult to convict, or if the reasonable doubt standard is somehow strengthened, you will protect both innocent and guilty defendants. There will be fewer wrongful convictions, but more wrongful acquittals.

If one of the costs of using the death penalty – wrongful conviction – is mitigated to some extent by the behavior of juries, it may also be the case that one of the benefits of the death penalty may be mitigated. If it is true that the harsher a sentence is for a given crime the lower will be the probability of conviction, there may exist a situation where increasing the severity of punishment may actually *lower* the expected punishment – the increase in severity is more than offset by the decrease in certainty due to the jury's behavior. Thus, it is possible that the death penalty can yield a smaller deterrent effect when compared to life imprisonment.

With advances in DNA testing there have been several well publicized reversals of convictions of defendants on Death Row. For example, in 1989 a Pennsylvania jury returned three death sentences against defendant Harold Wilson. In 2005, however, Wilson was acquitted of all charges because new DNA evidence revealed that blood from the crime scene did not come from him or any of the victims, indicating the involvement of another individual (Associated Press, November 18, 2005). Such reversals have been touted as strong arguments against the death penalty, as they point to the number of wrongfully convicted defendants who may have been tragically executed. But in addition to facilitating exoneration for wrongfully convicted defendants, DNA testing is widely used to prove guilt. Thus, DNA testing may be used to improve the *accuracy* of criminal verdicts, and such testing may lead to a reduction in *both* wrongful convictions and wrongful acquittals. This suggests that, in future death penalty cases, the possibility of wrongful conviction may be lowered, reducing one of the most severe costs associated with capital punishment *without* also reducing the possible benefit of the deterrent effect.

Furthermore, supporters of the death penalty often stress that there is substantial difference between wrongful conviction and wrongful *execution*. The criminal justice system is designed to allow defendants who are convicted of a capital crime ample opportunity to appeal their cases. In addition, there are numerous anti-death penalty groups who aid defendants in deferring or avoiding execution. Due to the severity of the sanction of capital punishment, there may be more wrongful convictions that are overturned than would be the case with the maximum sentence being life imprisonment. Thus, the imposition of the death penalty may reduce the probability of wrongful conviction not only at the trial stage, but also at the post-trial stage.

The other side of the story, however, is that, without the death penalty, there can *never* be a wrongful execution. But if you like to see economic reasoning pushed to the edge, consider the following counterargument to the wrongful execution criticism of the death penalty. *If* there is a deterrent effect to capital punishment, and an innocent defendant is wrongfully executed, there is even an up side to that tragic outcome: that execution will deter some murders, thus saving innocent lives. Keep in mind, however, that I am not arguing that innocent defendants should be purposely executed to create a deterrent effect. But if the death penalty is going to be used, and wrongful execution is an unavoidable cost, at least there is some offsetting benefit to that cost, regardless of how uncomfortable it is to consider that trade-off in terms of social policy.

Trial costs and the death penalty

In terms of implementation costs, it is often argued that the death penalty is a less costly punishment to impose compared to life imprisonment because, once the prisoner is put to death, that is the end of the punishment costs. And while this is true, critics argue that there are many other litigation costs to consider: a higher percentage of cases may go to trial when the death penalty is involved; death penalty cases tend to take longer to complete; jury selection is more complicated and time-consuming in a death penalty trial; death penalty trials tend to require more legal preparation; the sentencing phase of a death penalty trial is complex and lengthy; death penalty cases may have more lengthy and costly appeals; and so on. Furthermore, to the extent that execution occurs far into the future, imprisonment costs for a Death Row inmate are likely to be *at least* as large as they are for other inmates for a substantial amount of time.

In response to the observation that the death penalty is a more costly punishment to implement relative to life imprisonment, one pro-death penalty group offers the following comment: "This argument deserves no response; justice isn't up for sale to the lowest bidder" (*The New American*, 18 (11), 2002). This reasoning offers an excellent example of an issue I discussed in Chapter 1 – the identification and weighing of trade-offs in social policy debates. Ignoring the potential cost differences of the death penalty relative to life imprisonment is a subjective decision, which is the approach taken by the pro-death penalty group. Obviously, by ignoring a potential down side to the death penalty, it is more likely that one can conclude that the death penalty represents sound social policy. To the typical economist, however, that trade-off, having been identified, would not be ignored. The more important task would be to develop as accurate a measurement of the differential cost as possible, and then weigh those costs against all the other trade-offs that can be identified.

One other such trade-off has to do with the effect of the death penalty on the plea bargaining process. Plea bargaining is a crucial part of the criminal justice system, as it can allow a substantial savings in court costs. Prosecutors typically have the ability to offer two types of bargains to defendants. First, there is a *sentence* bargain, in which, for a given charge, the severity of the sentence is at issue. The prosecutor can encourage pleas by offering lower sentences. Second, there is a *charge* bargain, in which the prosecutor can offer to reduce the charge, and in turn reduce the severity of the sentence. The two bargains may differ in that, with a sentence charge, there may be a minimum sentence that constrains the bargaining, but, with a charge bargain, a lower charge may allow for a sentence that falls short of the higher charge's minimum. With the threat of a death penalty sentence, however, a defendant may be more likely to accept a plea bargain to avoid the harsh punishment. Furthermore, a defendant willing to accept a plea bargain may be willing to accept a harsher sentence than would be accepted without the threat of the death penalty. Thus, it is argued, prosecutors have a powerful bargaining tool to use when the death penalty is a viable option.

Although there is very little empirical evidence on the role of the death penalty in affecting plea bargains, there is one relatively recent study that attempts to shed some light on the issue (Kuziemko, 2006). In 1995, New York state reinstated capital punishment, yet many prosecutors publicly refused to seek the death penalty. Because other prosecutors welcomed back the death penalty, the study was able to compare the role of the death penalty in affecting plea bargains across two types of prosecutorial regimes. The study finds that the threat of the death penalty encourages more sentence bargains but not more charge bargains, and it appears to affect the *terms* of the plea bargain but not the *propensity* of the defendant to accept a plea bargain. Defendants most likely to accept a plea bargain do so with or without the death penalty, but they are willing to accept harsher sentences when the threat of the death penalty looms over them. Defendants least likely to plead out are not persuaded to avoid trial and accept reduced charges because of the death penalty. As a result, this one study concludes that the death penalty does not reduce the total number of cases that proceed to trial and does not increase the efficiency of plea bargains by reducing trial costs.

It is important to keep in mind, though, that any argument that involves the benefits of the death penalty as a *threat* to encourage plea bargains, must acknowledge that a threat in and of itself has little meaning if it is not credible. If defendants believe, as is typically the case, that the death penalty will rarely be enforced, there should be little effect on the plea bargaining process. Perhaps this partly helps explains the study's main result.

Race and capital punishment

Although I deal in more detail with racial issues in the criminal justice system in the next chapter, I will address the possibility of racial discrimination in the application of the death penalty here. To the extent that minorities are discriminated against during the sentencing or execution phase of death penalty cases, from a social policy perspective this may provide a strong argument against the use of capital punishment. But what is the evidence that racial discrimination occurs in death penalty cases? There have been several economic studies that have attempted to address this question.

One study (Argys and Mocan, 2004) examines the fate of prisoners who have already been sentenced to death and are awaiting execution. In any given year, there are several potential transitions a Death Row inmate can experience: they can be executed; they can die of other causes; they can have their sentence commuted to a lesser sentence; or, they can have their conviction or sentence overturned. It is also possible for the inmate simply to remain on death row. Using the entire population of inmates on Death Row between 1977 and 1997, the authors, as part of their study, analyze the effect of a prisoner's race on the different transition rates.

Their main result with respect to race is that African-American inmates (and other minorities) face a lower transition rate to execution and higher transition rate to commutation than do white inmates. Although these results suggest possible racial bias against white inmates, the source of this bias may be attributed to preferential treatment of whites in earlier stages of the legal process. It is possible that African-American defendants faced racial bias at the arrest, trial, conviction, or sentencing phases that led to Death Row incarceration. The favorable transition rates for African-American inmates may be a way for the authorities to counterbalance past prejudicial behavior on the part of the police, prosecutors, jurors, judges, or anyone else who had any impact on the defendant's path to Death Row.

Another possible explanation for the favorable transition rates for African-Americans involves discrimination based on the race of the *victims* of crime. In death penalty cases, it appears, defendants who murder white victims are treated more harshly than defendants who murder African-American victims. Because it is a fact that the majority of murders involve same-race defendants and victims, minority defendants may be treated more leniently because of the race of their victims, as opposed to their own race.

One study (Blume, Eisenberg and Wells, 2004) uses the racial relationship between defender and victim to account for the following fact. Looking at thirty-one states with more than ten Death Row inmates between the years 1977 and 1999, the authors observe that only three states (California, Nevada, and Utah) have a proportion of African-American Death Row inmates that exceeds the proportion of African-American offenders. In all other states the opposite is true. For example, in Alabama, 52.7 percent of the Death Row population is African-American, yet 69.1 percent of the offenders are African-American. Using national data, the authors find that African-Americans account for approximately 51.5 percent of murders, but only approximately 41.3 percent of death row inmates. The authors conclude that African-Americans are *under* represented on Death Row. But precisely why is this the case?

The authors identify two offsetting effects. First, African-Americans tend to be *under*represented on Death Row in black victim cases. Second, African-Americans tend to be *over*represented on Death Row in white victim cases. For example, between 1977 and 2000 in the state of Georgia, there were 7,091 murders involving same race African-American offender and victim, and 0.45 percent of the offenders were sentenced to death. There were 2,734 murders involving same-race white offender and victim, and 4.17 percent of the offenders were sentenced to death. There were 726 murders involving African-American offender and white victim, and 9.92 percent of the offenders were sentenced to death. Finally, there were 187 murders involving white offender and African-American victim, and 2.14 percent of the offenders were sentenced to death. In terms of ranking the race combinations and proportion of offenders sentenced to death, African-American murdering white is the highest, followed by white murdering white, white murdering African-American, and the lowest is African-American murdering African-American.

It appears, then, at least in Georgia (which is reasonably representative of many other states), the race of the victim is an important factor affecting the probability of being sentenced to death. African-American offenders are underrepresented on death row because only 0.45 percent of their same race murders have the offender sentenced to death. On the other hand, African-American offenders are overrepresented on death row because 9.92 percent of their different race murders have the offender sentenced to death. But when the two effects are combined, the first dominates the second because there are far more African-American same-race murders (7,091) than there are African-American offender and white victim murders (726). In all, the authors conclude that African-American offenders are underrepresented on Death Row because intraracial murders are far more common than interracial murders, and the reluctance to impose a death sentence on African-Americans who murder African-Americans outweighs the eagerness to impose a death sentence on African-Americans who murder whites.

Another study (Kubik and Moran, 2003) examines the effect of gubernatorial elections on the execution rate. They ask an interesting political question: Do "tough on crime" platforms during election campaigns lead to more executions? One substantial advantage an incumbent governor has over a potential political rival is that the incumbent has the authority to act on policy decisions. The rival, on the other hand, can only promise to act in a certain way once elected. The study finds that states are 25 percent more likely to carry out executions in a gubernatorial election year than in other years, and that elections have a larger effect on increasing the probability that an African-American defendant will be executed compared to the probability that a white defendant will be executed.

In addition to bias based on the defendant's or victim's race, there is also the possibility of bias based on the race of a juror. Compared to whites, are African-Americans more or less likely to vote for death during the sentencing phase of a capital punishment case? One study (Eisenberg, Garvey and Wells, 2001) attempts to answer this question. There may be many reasons why jurors vote the way they do in death penalty cases, but the trick is to sort through these reasons to isolate the effect of race on voting behavior.

For example, it is likely that the most important factor affecting how jurors vote is the factual strength of the case – the stronger the case the more likely are jurors to impose the death penalty. Using juror survey data from fifty-three capital cases in South Carolina between 1986 and 1997, the authors have information on how jurors perceived the strength of the cases in which they were involved. This allows the authors to provide some control for the strength of the case by including variables measuring the seriousness of the crime, the defendant's remorse, and the defendant's future dangerousness. With these controls, the empirical analysis can try to isolate the effect of juror race on the vote for capital punishment abstracting away from strength of case effects.

One significant complicating factor remains. When voting to impose the death penalty, jurors must reach a *unanimous* decision. If jurors must be in complete agreement, there are no differences in how they vote that can easily be attributed to any personal biases. But the authors find a clever way around this problem by examining how each juror votes *at first* during deliberation, and then how each juror *ultimately* votes. The argument is that if a juror's personal characteristics affect how they vote, these characteristics are likely to show themselves in a first vote before the jurors undertake deliberation to overcome any disagreements that may exist. Indeed, the study finds that, compared to African-Americans, whites are 20 percent more likely to vote for death on the first vote. Because mostly every case ends with a unanimous vote either for or against imposing the death penalty, racial distinctions typically wash out as a final decision is reached. Yet that still isn't the end of the story.

When the first vote is not unanimous, and the final vote is unanimous (as opposed to a deadlocked hung jury), the final vote almost always matches the decision of the initial majority. This suggests that the first vote is a primary predictor of the final vote. In the study's data set, African-Americans rarely make up a majority of jurors. If whites make up the majority of jurors, and they are more likely to vote for death than are African-Americans, the study concludes that juror racial bias does play a role in affecting the outcome of capital cases. In fact, the study confirms that the (believed to be) common practice of prosecutors seeking to empanel white jurors and defense attorneys seeking to empanel African-American jurors fits well into a model of rational trial behavior on the part of lawyers.

Final thoughts: Does deterrence really matter?

In all of the above discussion, I identified several potential costs of using the death penalty rather than life imprisonment. These included wrongful conviction costs, administrative, implementation, and legal costs, and possible racial discrimination costs. As far as the benefits of the death penalty, I identified only one – the deterrent effect. For each convicted murderer put to death, several innocent lives may be saved if the harsh punishment deters criminals from committing murder. But what if the deterrent effect does not exist? Can economic reasoning be used to examine alternative justifications for the death penalty?

Two of the most often stated benefits of the death penalty involve the concepts of justice and revenge. Some may argue that, to satisfy a sense of justice, the taking of a life demands the taking of a life in return – make the punishment fit the crime. As for revenge, the victim's family and friends may not be satisfied until retribution is taken. Both of these arguments have merit in that some individuals benefit when capital punishment is imposed on convicted murderers. These benefits, however, are usually psychological in nature and are difficult, if not impossible, to quantify. Furthermore, countering these psychological benefits are psychological costs incurred by individuals who believe that the death penalty is an overly harsh punishment. Social policy can certainly be based upon a consideration of psychological costs and benefits, but such policy is likely to be highly contentious, even more so than is often the case.

Why the deterrent effect is important to consider is because, at its core, it is a benefit that can *potentially* be quantified. Economic studies can attempt to measure the life–life trade-off, yielding a ratio of lives saved through deterrence relative to lives taken through capital punishment. But, as emphasized in this chapter, economists have not reached a consensus as to whether the deterrent effect of the death penalty is an empirical reality. Many conclusions have been reached by equally passionate and sincere scholars: the deterrent effect has been empirically verified; it has not been empirically verified; or, it has not been verified, but it may exist if the death penalty was implemented more often and in a more timely manner. In all, important as it is to consider the deterrent effect, it is equally important to keep in mind what is quoted at the beginning of this chapter – there is profound uncertainty in the economic literature as to whether the deterrent effect truly exists. In my opinion, any impartial reading of the literature *as a whole* can lead only to that conclusion.

Notes

Pioneering economic empirical research on confirming the deterrent effect of capital punishment is by Ehrlich (1975, 1977). A flurry of more recent papers that have confirmed Ehrlich's results are by Mocan and Gittings (2003, 2006), Dezhbakhsh, Rubin, and Shepherd (2003), Shepherd (2004, 2005), Zimmerman (2004), Dezhbakhsh and Shepherd (2006), and Ekelund, Jackson, Ressler, and Tollison (2006). Although not specifically a paper on capital punishment, Leamer (1983) uses death penalty data to demonstrate how difficult it is to confidently confirm the deterrent effect. The paper by Katz, Levitt and Shustorovich (2003) on the deterrent effect of the quality of prison life (discussed in the previous chapter) also finds little systematic evidence that the execution rate influences crime rates. Finally, an important and extraordinarily thorough study that confirms Leamer's basic conclusion is by Donohue and Wolfers (2005).

For an interesting debate on the moral aspects of capital punishment, see the papers by Sunstein and Vermeule (2005a, b), and Steiker (2005).

The material on the probability of conviction depending on the severity of the sanction can be found in Andreoni (1991). Papers on wrongful conviction costs are by Volokh (1997) and Lando (2006). The Volokh paper offers an interesting and entertaining discussion of the Blackstone Ratio (the ratio of acceptable wrongful acquittals relative to wrongful convictions) and its many refinements over time. A study of plea bargaining and the death penalty is by Kuziemko (2006). Other papers that deal with prosecutorial discretion and the outcomes of trials (but not explicitly about the death penalty) are by Elder (1989), Kessler and Piehl (1998), and Glaesr, Kessler and Piehl (2000).

Papers on race and the death penalty are by Langbein (1999), Eisenberg, Garvey, and Wells (2001), Spurr (2002), Kubik and Moran (2003), Argys and Mocan (2004), Baldus and Woodworth (2004), and Blume, Eisenberg, and Wells (2004).

5 Race and crime

Although racial discrimination in applying the death penalty (discussed in the previous chapter) is one of the most prevalent topics when examining the issue of crime and race, economists have studied several other aspects of possible racial discrimination in the criminal justice system. This chapter reviews some of the studies that examine such topics as racial profiling, discrimination in sentencing convicted criminals, discrimination in setting bail, and how criminal background checks affect the employment opportunities of minorities.

Racial profiling

It is an empirical fact that when the police stop motorists to determine if they are carrying illegal drugs, African-Americans are far more likely to be searched than are white motorists. On Interstate 95 in Maryland during the last half of the 1990s, African-Americans made up 63 percent of the motorists searched, yet made up only 18 percent of the motorists on the road (Knowles, Persico and Todd, 2001). At first blush, this appears to be a troubling fact supporting the existence of racial bias on the part of the police, but there may be an alternative explanation. If the objective of the police is to maximize successful searches, *and* if race can be used as a predictor of criminal behavior (because it is correlated with other more difficult to observe predictors), racial profiling may be an efficient policing technique. In the economics literature, racial profiling used to predict criminal behavior is referred to as *statistical* discrimination, while racial profiling that is motivated by prejudice is referred to as *preference-based* discrimination. Is there a way to distinguish between the two?

One important study (Knowles, Persico and Todd, 2001) provides the groundwork for the economic approach to racial profiling. The authors develop a clever theoretical model of profiling that guides their empirical approach to distinguishing between statistical and preference-based discrimination. While their model is necessarily technical and abstract, its core intuition is fairly accessible. Furthermore, the authors fully exploit the concept of rational crime analysis by assuming rational behavior on the part of the criminals and the police. Thus, the model is worth discussing in some detail.

Consider two groups of individuals – group A and group B – that can be distinguished by some easily observable characteristic, such as race. In both groups, a certain percentage of individuals carry illegal drugs. The objective of the police is to maximize the number of successful searches, known as *hits*, taking into account the cost of searching. Let's begin by assuming that the police are equally likely to search both groups. In that case, the group that has the higher percentage of individuals who carry illegal drugs (let's say group A) will yield more successful searches. Equally likely searches, then, can yield different hit rates. If the police are not racially biased, a more efficient use of resources would be to search group A more intensively relative to Group B to increase the overall number of hits. But how will the criminals in each group respond to the change in search rates?

As the police intensify the search of group A there will be a greater deterrent effect and less criminal activity in that group, but a smaller deterrent effect and more criminal activity in group B. As the hit rate in group A begins to decline, and the hit rate in group B continues to rise, eventually the two hit rates will equalize. If not, the police will continue to have an incentive to move more resources toward searching the group with the higher hit rate. Thus, if criminals respond to the changes in deterrence, equal hit rates between the two groups are an indication that the police are *not* racially biased, even if the search rates between the groups are different. If the police are racially biased, however, we can expect to see a *lower* hit rate associated with the group that suffers the prejudice. In other words, the lower hit rate indicates that the police are inefficiently overdeterring that group, suggesting that an additional explanation, such as racial bias, is partly motivating the searches.

A real-world example can help illustrate the main idea behind the theoretical model. A case was brought against the United States Customs Service and some of its employees for supposed discriminatory practices at O'Hare Airport in the late 1990s. The case was filed by a group of African-American women who had been subjected to non-routine searches, such as x-rays and strip searches, yet no contraband was found on any of the women. The claim against the customs officials was that they acted with bias against African-American women over other groups, including white men, white women, and African-American men.

To bolster their claim, the plaintiffs presented data from a government report on the searching of airline passengers. That report found that, based on their sample (using national data), 6.4 percent of African-American women were subjected to x-rays, compared to only 0.73 percent of white women, 0.53 percent of white men, and 4.6 percent of African-American men. Based solely on these search rates, then, African-American women were nearly nine times more likely to be searched compared to white women, twelve times more likely compared to white men, and approximately one and a half times more likely compared to African-American men. Especially when compared to white men and women, African-American women faced substantially higher search rates. Are these differential search rates evidence of racial bias? To answer this question, we need to examine the hit rates.

For the sample of airline passengers used in the study, contraband was found on 27.6 percent of African-American women, 19.5 percent of white women, 25.1 percent of white men, and 61.6 percent of African-American men. The plaintiffs' interpretation of these hit rates is that the substantially greater search rates for African-American women were not matched by substantially greater hit rates, implying that the excessive searching was ineffective and biased. But the similar hit rates between African-American women, white women, and white men suggest a *lack* of bias between these three groups. If the excessive searching of African-American women was biased, we would expect to see lower hit rates for that group because a criterion other than crime deterrence would be influencing the authorities' decision to search and a large number of innocent airline passengers would be ineffectively searched.

In dismissing the complaint, the judge in this case specifically referred to economic research on racial profiling, and offered the following observations on the data presented by the plaintiffs:

> Data from the [government's] report do not imply that Customs officials are searching black women (or any other group) but not similarly situated passengers in other groups. The report's [evidence] shows that Customs officials search black women with (on average) the same degree of suspicion that leads them to search white women or white men. A 27.6 percent success rate for a particular kind of border search is not to be sneezed at. It may imply that the Customs officials are conducting too few searches, not too many.
>
> (*Anderson v. Cornejo*, 355 F. 3d 1021, at 1024–1025)

Actually, any evidence of bias based on those hit rates suggests that it is African-American women, white women, and white men who are being biased against relative to African-American men. The hit rate is so high for African-American men that it appears that a more efficient use of resources would be to increase the intensity of search of that group while reducing the intensity of search of the other three groups (taken as a whole). Recall that differentially low hit rates imply possible bias. For the group of passengers used in the study, it is white women who have the lowest hit rate and, therefore, may be suffering the most bias.

In the original economic study, the authors use motor vehicle searches in Maryland to develop their data set. When considering the police's objective of maximizing the number of hits, they find little difference between the hit rates for African-Americans and whites. This leads them to conclude that there is no evidence of preference-based discrimination in their data. They also consider a slightly different objective for the police – maximizing the number of hits that involve a "large" amount of drugs. With this definition, they find that African-Americans have a higher hit rate than do whites, suggesting that it is the group of white motorists who are being biased against. In all, their conclusion is that their data do not yield evidence of racial bias against African-American motorists.

While the authors of the original model offer an important starting point for the economic analysis of racial profiling, researchers that follow develop theoretical refinements and present empirical evidence that challenge the initial findings. The theoretical refinements challenge the idea that if the police are not racially biased in their searches of different groups, hit rates between the groups will be the same. In other words, equal hit rates may actually imply preference-based discrimination. The technical reasons behind this refinement are difficult to explain (they involve introducing into the model heterogeneity among police officers in their costs of search or preferences for discrimination, or heterogeneity among potential search victims in their costs and benefits from criminal behavior), so I will briefly focus on the empirical findings.

Another way to empirically investigate the existence of bias associated with racial profiling is to distinguish *police officers* by race, as opposed to just distinguishing the victims of search by race. If the police are not racially biased when they search individuals, African-American and white police officers should approach racial profiling in similar ways. If there is an efficient unequal search rate for two groups of individuals, any police officer with a non-biased objective, regardless of race, should be applying the same technique. But if the race of a police officer affects the rate of search, this is an indication of possible racial bias. Do white police officers excessively search African-American individuals? Do African-American police officers excessively search white individuals?

Three studies examining the search of motorists attempt to answer these questions. The first study (Antonovics and Knight, 2004) finds that the race of the police officer does have an effect on search rates. If the race of the officer is different than the race of the motorist, there is a higher probability that the motorist will be searched. This holds for white officers searching African-American motorists, and African-American officers searching white motorists. After ruling out a couple of other explanations, the authors conclude that they find evidence of racially biased profiling. A second study (Close and Mason, 2006) confirms the results of the previous study. The authors find that while white drivers are subject to favorable bias from white police officers and no bias from African-American or Latino officers, African-American and Latino drivers are subjected to punitive bias from white officers. A third study (Anwar and Fang, 2006) also finds that the race of the police officer has an effect on search rates, but they cannot strongly conclude based on their results that the different search rates are racially biased.

In all, the evidence is strong that different groups of individuals, often distinguished by race, face very different search rates by the authorities. Racial profiling does exist. The key contribution of economic reasoning, however, is to emphasize that different search rates, even substantially different search rates, are not necessarily an indication of racial bias. Some studies conclude that racial profiling is an efficient police search technique that involves statistical discrimination. Other studies conclude that racial profiling involves preference-based discrimination. It may simply be the case that racial profiling involves both types of discrimination. Policy officials, then, face the difficult task of determining if the benefits of racial profiling as an effective police search technique outweigh the costs associated with racially biased police behavior.

Discrimination in sentencing

How does the race of the defendant affect the severity of the punishment in terms of prison sentences? Glaeser and Sacerdote (2003) examine the role of victim race in affecting the punishment of drivers convicted of vehicular homicide. Such crimes are largely caused by drivers who are under the influence of alcohol or drugs, and as a result have more in common with accidents than they do with intentional acts of violence. This allows us to think of the victims of vehicular homicide to be largely determined at random, especially when compared to victims of other violent crimes. The cleverness behind the study stems from the fact that the more complicated the relationship between criminal and victim the more factors exist that may affect punishment. Sorting out the different factors to attribute differential punishments to bias becomes a difficult task. With randomly selected victims, however, the relationship between criminal and victim is far less complicated. If victims of vehicular homicide can truly be thought of as being randomly selected, differential punishments can more confidently be attributed to the presence of bias.

The results of the study are not encouraging in terms of ruling out bias as playing a significant role in determining the severity of punishment. The main result in terms of racial bias is that drivers who kill African-Americans receive sentences that are approximately 60 percent shorter than the sentences received by drivers who kill whites. In terms of gender bias, drivers who kill women receive sentences that are approximately 60 percent longer than those received by drivers who kill men. Furthermore, the study finds that there is no difference in the role of victim effects between vehicular homicide and other types of murder. The study concludes that bias appears to be an important contributing factor in the determination of punishment.

Another study (Mustard, 2001b) examines possible bias in sentencing for criminal cases tried in U.S. federal courts. In 1984, the United States Sentencing Commission reformed the federal sentencing guidelines to eliminate disparities in sentencing explicitly relating to the defendant's race, gender, ethnic background, and income. The guidelines allow for two main components in determining a sentence: the severity of the defendant's offense; and, the defendant's criminal history, including the number and severity of past offenses, and prison time served. With this information, the guidelines present sentence ranges that judges are to use.

The author presents an example of how the guidelines are used to determine a sentence range for a particular crime. For the offense of mishandling toxic substances, the base offense level is eight points. If there was an ongoing discharge of a toxic substance into the environment, an additional six points are added. If the offense created a substantial risk of death or serious injury, another nine points are added. Thus, the base offense and the two additional aggravating factors lead to an offense level of twenty-three points. As for the criminal history score, the categories range from 1 to 6, with 6 being the highest. If the criminal committed the offense while under any criminal justice sentence (including probation, parole, and so on), and/or incurred previous sanctions, the criminal history score would be positively affected. Let's say this particular criminal has a criminal history score of 3, and an offense level of twenty-three points. The guidelines recommend a sentence range of fifty-seven to seventy-one months. However, these ranges are not set in stone. First of all, because they are sentence *ranges*, judges have some discretion in determining sentence length and still abiding by the guidelines. Second, judges are given some discretion in sentencing outside of the ranges, allowing for more or less severe punishments than the guidelines dictate.

To demonstrate whether judges display bias when using their discretion, the study takes advantage of a data set that is made up of over 77,000 individuals sentenced under the guidelines between October 1991 and September 1994, across forty-one criminal offenses. The author tries to explain the variation in the defendants' sentences, and has data pertaining to each defendant's offense level, criminal history, race, education, income, number of dependants, and citizenship (U.S. or not). At first blush, the data demonstrate that African-Americans and Hispanics face, on average, longer sentences than whites, and that men face longer sentences than women. But this is not taking into account the defendants' offense levels and criminal history scores, which are both larger for minorities over whites, and for men over women.

After controlling for defendants' offense level and criminal history, and for the district court in which they are tried, the study's main result is that large disparities in sentence length exist on the basis of race, gender, education, income, and citizenship. In other words, similar defendants, in terms of where they are tried and what the guidelines dictate their sentence range to be, face very different sentences based on characteristics the guidelines are supposed to rule out. African-Americans tend to face harsher sentences than whites, men face harsher sentences than women, defendants with low levels of education and low levels of income face harsher sentences compared to better educated and wealthier defendants, and non-U.S. citizens face harsher sentences than U.S. citizens. The author also finds that a majority of the sentence differences stem from departures from the guidelines, as opposed to variations within the stated sentence ranges. The study concludes that judges appear to routinely ignore the dictated sentence ranges and impose their own biases upon the sentencing procedure.

Discrimination in setting bail

In June, 2006, five African-American defendants filed a multimillion-dollar lawsuit claiming discrimination by the Butte County (California) criminal justice system. As part of their claim, they argued that excessive bail was set in their particular cases, especially compared to white defendants charged with similar crimes. One study (Ayres and Waldfogel, 1994) attempts to examine racial bias in the criminal justice system by determining whether there is a difference in how bail is set for minority versus white defendants.

When judges set bail, there are many factors that can be considered in determining the amount to impose on a particular defendant. But, at its core, the role of bail is to assure that the defendant appears in court when required. If a defendant does not appear, the bail is forfeited, either directly by the defendant or by a bail bondsman. Thus, the reasoning goes, the greater the amount of bail the greater is the incentive for the defendant to appear in court, or for the bail bondsman to guarantee that the defendant appears in court. If bail is set *without* regard to racial bias, different bail amounts should primarily reflect only differences in defendant flight risks, with higher bail amounts reflecting higher flight risks. If bail is set with racial bias, minority defendants with equal flight risks to white defendants may, nevertheless, face higher bail amounts.

Before turning to the empirical results, it is worth highlighting the key elements of the authors' model of bail setting. Consider a defendant who has a probability of flight risk that is inversely related to the amount of bail that is set by the court. The higher the bail, the lower will be the defendant's flight risk. The objective of a judge in their model is to set an amount of bail that yields a desired flight risk. Furthermore, that desired flight risk should be the same for all defendants.

Assume there is a high-flight-risk defendant (defendant A) and a low-flight-risk defendant (defendant B). This means that, if both defendants face the same bail amount, A is more likely to flee than is B. If the goal of a judge is to insure a constant desired flight risk across both defendants, A must face a higher bail amount than does B. For example, assume that if bail is set at $5,000 for each defendant, A's flight risk is 20 percent and B's flight risk is 15 percent. If the desired flight risk for each defendant is 10 percent, the judge must set a higher bail for A than B, and both bail amounts must exceed $5,000. So, maybe the appropriate bail amounts to assure a 10 percent flight risk are $10,000 for A and $7,500 for B. Although these bail amounts differ, the difference cannot be explained by judicial bias. The difference in the bail amounts reflect true differences in the flight risks of the defendants. But now let's say that defendant A is a minority defendant, and defendant B is not. If judicial racial bias does exist, it is possible that A's bail may be set at an amount that exceeds $10,000, such as $12,500, and the additional $2,500 cannot be explained by the differences in A's and B's flight risks.

Using data from criminal cases in New Haven, Connecticut, for the year 1990, the study examines the effect of race on the level of bail, controlling for several other factors, especially those relating to the nature and severity of the crime. The data set consists of 1,366 defendants, made up of approximately 19 percent white men, 53 percent African-American men, 11 percent Hispanic men, and 17 percent women of all three races. The most common offenses involve drugs, assault, disorderly conduct, and larceny, but there are several other less frequent offenses. The average bail amount is $3,466, and the average fee paid to bail bondsmen is $177.

The study's main finding is that race does statistically significantly affect bail, with African-American men facing (on average) 35 percent higher bail than white men, and Hispanic men facing (on average) 19 percent higher bail than white men. The problem with these empirical results, however, is that due to data limitations the regression equation does not include many other factors that could affect the determination of bail. Such factors include the weight of the evidence against the defendant, the defendant's prior criminal record and prior court appearance record, the defendant's employment record, and so on. The fewer relevant factors that can be controlled in the regression equation the less confident we are that the racial bias effect is accurately accounting for differences in bail amounts.

To circumvent the omitted variables problem, the authors present a novel idea. Instead of looking at differences in bail amounts to test for racial bias, they look at differences in the bail bond *rates* bail bondsmen charge to their customers. If a defendant uses a bail bondsman, it is the bondsman who puts up the bail and charges the defendant a percentage fee. Although there are regulations that govern the setting of bond rates, bondsmen do have the opportunity to vary rates across defendants. What the authors find is that bond rates are *lower* for minorities than they are for whites. Surprisingly, they interpret this result as suggesting that racial bias *against* minorities does exist in the setting of bail. How do they reach this conclusion?

A defendant who uses the services of a bail bondsman agrees to pay a percentage rate of the bail amount to have the bondsman put up the bail. If the defendant does not appear, the bondsman forfeits the bail amount (or in some cases, a portion of the amount). This provides the bondsman with an incentive to assure that the defendant does not flee. For example, a bond dealer who has $50,000 at risk if a defendant fails to appear is likely going to devote more resources to monitoring the defendant's whereabouts and, if necessary, searching to reapprehend the defendant, compared to a bond dealer who only has $10,000 at risk. The more likely a defendant is to flee, then, the more costly (in terms of flight risk) it is for the bondsman to put up the bail for the defendant.

If we assume that the bail bonds market is fairly competitive and individual bondsmen face similar costs in operating their businesses, we can expect that differences in bond rates across defendants are largely due only to differences in flight risks. Quite simply, defendants who have higher flight risks are expected to face higher bond rates than defendants who have lower flight risks. If, as the authors find, minority defendants face lower bond rates than do white defendants, it must be because minority defendants have lower flight risks. So the last piece of the puzzle is to explain why this may be so.

Let's return to the numerical example introduced above. With defendant A's bail set at $10,000, and defendant B's set at $7,500, we assumed that these bail amounts would equalize the flight risks between the defendants at 10 percent. The difference in the bail amounts can be explained by the difference in flight risks *before* bail was set – defendant A had a higher flight risk. If the judge's objective is to set bail to equalize flight risk, the defendants have the same flight risk *after* the bail is set. It is after the bail is set that the defendants seek a bail bondsman. With equal flight risks at that time, the bond rates should be very similar between the defendants. But if bail is set at $12,500 for the minority defendant, the increased bail lowers that defendant's flight risk, thus lowering the bond rate that can be charged. If minority defendants face lower bond rates, it must be because they have lower flight risks, which must be because their bail is set at too high a level, which suggests the possibility of racial bias in the setting of bail.

What's clever about this study is that the authors look at the bail bonds market to examine potential *judicial* bias. Trying to sort out why judges do what they do can be an empirical mess, as it can be impossible to distinguish between subjective values that vary from judge to judge. By focusing on the *bail* bonds market, competitive *bail* bondsmen must survive by setting bond rates that are neither too high nor too low relative to their rivals. And the authors find that the bail bonds market in New Haven is indeed competitive, especially compared to other Connecticut towns. They identify eight active *bail* bond dealers in New Haven whose average bond rates are 64 percent of the statutory maximum, compared to other towns with only one or two *bail* bond dealers, whose average rates are typically 99 percent of the statutory maximum. They attribute the lower rates charged in New Haven primarily to the larger number of firms competing there.

If competitive market conditions force bond rates to vary primarily due to differences in flight risks, and these differences are primarily due to differences in bail amounts, more confidence can be placed on this approach in identifying judicial racial bias. Of course, the authors correctly point out that there still may be other factors accounting for the differences in bond rates that are not due to judicial bias, but their approach offers an excellent starting point.

Race and criminal background checks

Another interesting racial issue involves the potential for employer discrimination against minority job candidates who may or may not have criminal records. In general, independent of race, employers may be unwilling to hire workers who have criminal records. Such workers may be considered untrustworthy, or employers may be concerned about being liable for potential further criminal actions by these workers, or certain jobs may, by law, be unavailable to ex-offenders. Employers who are concerned about these problems may use criminal background checks to screen out workers they deem undesirable. While this may appear to be beneficial to employers, it makes it difficult for ex-offenders to find legitimate employment after release from prison. This additional roadblock into the legitimate work force may provide incentives to return to pursuing criminal activities. Thus, many argue that criminal background checks should be prohibited, or at least severely restricted, so that ex-offenders can be given a better chance to find legitimate employment. In effect, restricting the use of criminal background checks may be a useful social policy to help reduce crime.

Unfortunately, restricting the use of criminal background checks can encourage racial discrimination against minority workers, especially African-Americans. It is a striking fact that a fairly large portion of men in the United States serve some time in prison during their lifetime, with that portion being approximately 9 percent. But this portion can be segmented by race, with the numbers showing that 28 percent of African-American men, 16 percent of Hispanic men, and 4 percent of white men serve some time in prison (Holzer, Raphael and Stoll, 2006). If an employer is concerned about the criminal history of a potential employee, but *cannot* gain access to criminal records, the employer may decide to use the employee's race as a proxy for criminal history. With a large proportion of African-Americans who have served time, an employer may incorrectly exclude an African-American worker who does not have a criminal history. Thus, allowing for criminal background checks may *improve* the job prospects of minorities who have no criminal history.

This leaves us with two opposing effects. If criminal background checks are easy to perform, fewer minorities with criminal records may find employment, but minorities without criminal records may face better job market prospects. Conversely, if criminal background checks are difficult to perform, fewer minorities without criminal records may find employment if employers use race as a proxy for criminal history, but minorities with criminal records will face better job market prospects. In terms of social policy, then, the relevant question is: Does allowing employers easy access to criminal background checks improve or worsen the labor market prospects of minority workers?

One study (Holzer, Raphael and Stoll, 2006) attempts to provide an empirical answer to this question. The authors have access to survey data collected from over 3,000 firms in the Atlanta, Boston, Detroit, and Los Angeles metropolitan areas between June 1992 and May 1994. In their sample, approximately 32 percent of firms always perform criminal background checks for their applicants, 17 percent sometimes perform checks, and 51 percent never perform checks. Also, approximately 62 percent of the firms report that they will probably not or definitely not hire applicants with criminal backgrounds, and 38 percent report that they probably will or definitely will hire such applicants. Furthermore, this aversion to hiring workers with criminal backgrounds is much stronger than employer aversion to hiring workers with other potential stigmas, such as being a welfare recipient, having no high school diploma, having a spotty work history, and being unemployed for more than a year.

The main finding of the study is that employers who perform criminal background checks are more likely to hire African-American workers compared to employers that do not perform background checks. The improved job prospects of African-Americans who have no criminal history are found to more than offset the worsened prospects of those who have criminal records. Furthermore, the authors' data allow them to identify employers who indicate a strong aversion toward hiring ex-offenders, and they find that for this group (relative to employers who do not share this aversion) their main result is even stronger. They conclude that making it difficult for employers to perform criminal background checks may exacerbate racial discrimination in hiring practices and ultimately hurt more potential employees than it helps. They do correctly point out, however, that there will be ex-offenders, even those with minor criminal histories, who find that returning to the legitimate labor market will be difficult if background checks are easy to perform.

Other racial concerns

Due to the availability of data, most of the formal studies on racial issues in the U.S. criminal justice system focus on whites versus African-American or Hispanic defendants. There are, however, other groups who have claimed that they have faced racial bias, including Asian-Americans, Native Americans, and, especially since 9/11, Arab-Americans. For example, in an article entitled "The Slippery Slope of Racial Profiling," by Nicole Davis, a researcher at the Applied Research Center, she reports that the following criteria were used to stop, search, detain, and question a suspected terrorist:

> The profile of a terrorist is a man in his twenties or thirties who comes from Saudi Arabia, Egypt, or Pakistan. He probably lives in one of six states – Texas, New Jersey, California, New York, Michigan, or Florida. And he is likely to have engaged in some sort of suspicious activity, such as taking flying lessons, traveling, or getting a driver's license. Meeting one of these profiles is enough to get you questioned. Meeting all three is likely to land you in jail. Darrell Issa fit the profile. He is Arab-American, he is from California, and he was traveling to Saudi Arabia. The crew of his flight refused to allow him to board the plane.

Darrell Issa, by the way, was a U.S. Congressman at the time.

For an international example of claims of bias in the criminal justice system, I now turn to the case of the Aboriginal people in Australia. In 1991, a five-volume report entitled *The Royal Commission into Aboriginal Deaths in Custody* fueled a substantial public and academic discussion of possible reforms of the Australian criminal justice system. The main finding of the report was that the Aboriginal people were overrepresented in custody. Although it can be argued that this custodial overrepresentation was largely explained by the relatively high Aboriginal offense rate (for example, see Weatherburn, Fitzgerald and Hua, 2003), there are also claims of systemic bias in the criminal justice system. While the report recognizes that reforms to the criminal justice system are needed, that is not the main concern:

> Changes to the operation of the criminal justice system alone will not have a significant impact on the number of persons entering into custody or the number of those who die in custody; the social and economic circumstances which both predispose Aboriginal people to offend and which explain why the

criminal justice system focuses upon them are much more significant factors in over-representation.

(Cunneen, 2006, p. 335, from the Royal Commission report)

To address these concerns, the report put forth a total of 339 recommendations: 126 recommendations dealing with the underlying socioeconomic factors relating to overrepresentation; 106 recommendations dealing with the criminal justice system and overrepresentation; and, 107 recommendations dealing specifically with deaths in custody.

In response to the report, the Australian government allocated $400 million (Australian) in an attempt to implement many of the recommendations. Although approximately one-third of the recommendations involved reforms to the criminal justice system, only a small amount of funds was allocated toward reforms to policing, custodial arrangements, criminal law, judicial proceedings, and so on ($7.52 million, or 1.9 percent of the total). The greatest amount of funds was allocated toward Aboriginal drug and alcohol services ($71.6 million, or 17.9 percent), land acquisition and development programs ($60 million, or 15 percent), legal services ($50.4 million, or 12.6 percent), community development employment programs ($43.9 million, or 11 percent), and many other social programs relating to improved educational and employment opportunities (see Cunneen, 2006). How effective these reforms have been in alleviating Aboriginal overrepresentation remains an open question, but the Australian experience demonstrates the willingness of the authorities to at least recognize and address potential biases in the criminal justice system.

In all, considering the studies discussed in this and the previous chapter, there is a large body of evidence that suggests that race does play a role in the criminal justice system. But this role may not be an obvious one. With racial profiling, for example, distinguishing individuals by race may be an efficient policing technique. And while much evidence points to racial bias against minorities, some evidence (such as with the Death Row transition rates study in Chapter 4) finds racial bias against whites. The key contribution of economic analysis, however, is to emphasize that there may be non-discriminatory reasons to distinguish between defendants based on race, and care must be taken to sort out discriminatory from non-discriminatory distinctions.

Notes

The economic literature on racial profiling has exploded in recent years, largely due to the important paper by Knowles, Persico and Todd (2001). Empirical studies of racial profiling and its potential role as a preference-based or statistical discriminatory policing technique are by Donohue and Levitt (2001a), Leung, Wooley, Tremblay and Vitaro (2002), Antonovics and Knight (2004), Dharmapala and Ross (2004), Hernandez-Murillo and Knowles (2004), Persico and Todd (2004), Persico and Castleman (2005), Anwar and Fang (2006), Close and Mason (2006), Gelman, Fagan and Kiss (2006), Grogger and Ridgeway (2006), and Ridgeway (2006). More theoretical or discussion-based papers are by Beck and Daly (1999), Myers (2002), Persico (2002), Dominitz (2003), Bunzel and Marcoul (2005),

Durlauf (2005), Persico and Todd (2005), Todd (2005), Dominitz and Knowles (2006), and Bjerk (2007).

Other papers on racial discrimination and various aspects of the criminal justice system are by Mustard (2001b) and Glaeser and Sacerdote (2003) on sentencing, Ayres and Waldfogel (1994) on setting bail, Holzer, Raphael and Stoll (2006) on criminal background checks, Lott (2000) on affirmative action and police hiring, and Gyimah-Brempong and Price (2006) on discrimination based on African-American skin hue. Papers on Aboriginal issues in Australia are by Weatherburn, Fitzgerald and Hua (2003) and Cunneen (2006).

6 Private crime deterrence

Crime-fighting is not just for public authorities and superheroes. Ordinary citizens also devote a substantial amount of resources to deterring crime. Typical deterrence efforts often involve home security measures such as deadbolt locks, bars on windows, burglar alarms, fences, dogs, safes, weapons, and so on. Residents in certain communities may even act in concert by hiring private security officers to patrol the whole neighborhood. One study (Philipson and Posner, 1996) cites evidence that aggregate private expenditures on preventing crime in the United States are estimated to be $300 billion per year, while public expenditures on the criminal justice system are $90 billion per year, less than one-third the private amount. Although we may be very concerned with how public officials spend our tax dollars on crime deterrence, should we care at all about how private citizens spend their *own* dollars on deterrence?

Generally, when economists discuss private decisions to purchase goods and services, it boils down to a very simple premise: if an individual purchases a product, the value (or willingness to pay) for that product must exceed the price. If I buy a television set that costs $1,000, it must be the case that I value it at more than $1,000. Thus, I make myself better off by buying the set. If I don't value the television set at a minimum of $1,000, I am better off not buying the set. Whatever the case, it is not often that you hear scholars debate the role of public policy in either encouraging or discouraging individuals to buy television sets. Yet, when it comes to buying home security devices, there are scholars who examine the issue as to whether individuals are buying too many or too few of such devices. Why are these scholars concerned with private individuals' home security purchases?

Protecting personal property

It is simple to identify the primary motive of individuals who purchase home security devices – they want to prevent or reduce the amount of theft they face. If I put bars on my windows and expensive deadbolt locks on my doors, I'm concerned with keeping thieves out of *my* house, not out of my neighbor's house. Granted, I may not want my neighbor to be robbed, but that is not my main concern. Unfortunately, by making my house more secure I actually may be making it *more* likely that my neighbor will be robbed.

By putting bars on my windows I am clearly demonstrating to potential criminals that my house will be difficult to rob. Although some criminals may still find it worth while to' break into my house, others are likely to just move down the road to find easier targets. Thus, this particular investment in home security is likely to deter criminals from robbing my house, but it may not deter criminals from robbing someone else's house. In this case, crime may only be *diverted* as opposed to deterred.

When private security measures are *observable* by criminals, such as bars on windows, fences, loud dogs, and so on, crime may be redistributed from individuals with these measures to others who do not have these measures. In that case, the private benefits of observable security measures do not translate into social benefits. Costly resources are being used, yet crime in the aggregate is not being deterred.

On the other hand, there may be private security measures that are *unobservable* to criminals, or at least not easily observable. For example, I can install in my house a burglar alarm or a safe to store my valuables, and a criminal may not find out about these measures until they enter my house. These measures may not completely deter criminals from breaking into my house, but they will increase the costs to criminals of stealing from me. And the whole objective of crime deterrence measures, either public or private, is to increase the costs of crime to rational criminals. But, in addition, my unobservable private security measures may actually deter criminals from breaking into my *neighbor's* house.

If security measures are not easily observed, in deciding to commit a crime a criminal may take into account the increased costs that will be faced. Will a potential mugging victim be carrying a concealed weapon? Will an automobile have a hidden tracking device that will make it easier for the police to trace the location of the stolen car? Will a house have a silent alarm that alerts security officers if a break-in occurs? If a criminal can't precisely determine which victims have installed unobservable security devices, the criminal will confront a higher probability of facing such devices *regardless* of the identity of the victim. Thus, unobservable measures have the ability to deter crime, not just to divert it. Private security measures in this case yield private benefits that do translate into social benefits.

Taken together, from a social perspective it can be argued that private individuals *over*invest in observable security measures, but *under*invest in unobservable ones. Private observable measures yield private but not social benefits if crime is simply diverted from one victim to another. These resources are, in a social sense, wasted. Private unobservable measures, however, yield private and social benefits. But, from a private perspective, some individuals may not find it in their own best interest to invest in unobservable security measures even if such investment would be socially optimal. After all, if my neighbor can take an action to reduce the overall crime rate, why should I spend any extra to do so? By not taking into account the additional social benefit of one's actions, it may be the case that not enough resources are being devoted to private measures.

From a policy perspective, some economists argue that a possible role for social intervention is to discourage (or at least not encourage) observable private security measures, but encourage unobservable ones. Precisely how that can be done remains an interesting question. While there is very little empirical evidence on the diversion or deterrent effects of private security measures, there is one study (Ayres and Levitt, 1998) that examines such effects in terms of automobile theft.

In 1986 the Lojack Company introduced a radio transmitter tracking device (referred to simply as Lojack) that can be installed in cars. If a car with Lojack is stolen, the police can remotely activate the transmitter and track the movement and location of the stolen vehicle. Massachusetts was the first state in which Lojack was used, and by 1994 (the end date for the study's sample period) a dozen other states followed suit. Lojack provides an excellent setting in which to test the effect on the crime rate of private security measures.

First, Lojack truly is a private security measure. New car buyers can pay a one-time fee at the time of purchase to have the device installed. Second, Lojack is an unobservable security measure. Lojack can be hidden in one of many places on a car. As a condition for the Lojack company to be allowed entry into a market, the authorities require Lojack not to be identifiable in any specific automobile. Furthermore, insurance boards allow for insurance premium discounts only if owners do not identify the existence of Lojack. Third, Lojack is predicted to deter auto theft by allowing the police to more quickly locate stolen cars and possibly apprehend thieves, and, more important, to locate and shut down "chop shops" where the stolen cars are disassembled. Also, to the extent that car thieves are repeat offenders, the incapacitation effect of prison can further lower the crime rate. Finally, as an unobservable security measure, Lojack is predicted to offer little deterrence value to the owner of a car. The private benefits of Lojack are found in higher retrieval rates and lower damage rates of stolen cars, and not in lowering the probability that a *specific* car is stolen in the first place.

The empirical results of the study are quite striking. It is found that for every three Lojacks that are installed, one auto theft is deterred. Furthermore, this deterrent effect does not depend on wide use of Lojack. Because Lojack is available for new cars only, typically less than 2 percent of registered vehicles in a covered market are equipped with the device. But by increasing the probability of *any* new car having the device, auto thieves face higher costs of crime and appear to be deterred by Lojack.

As for the diversion effect, the study attempts to measure three types of crime displacement that may be brought about by Lojack. First, there is no evidence to suggest that auto thieves are substituting between markets with Lojack and markets without Lojack. Second, the introduction of Lojack does not appear to increase crime rates of other crimes, such as burglary, robbery, assault, murder, and so on. Finally, the one diversion effect that is found is increased car theft of older cars, which are far less likely to have the Lojack device installed. This diversion effect, however, is small compared to the deterrent effect.

The study also addresses other possible effects that may explain the lower auto theft crime rate. When Lojack is introduced into a market, it may coincide with an increased police effort to fight auto theft. There may also be other precautions car owners take to deter theft. If there are additional public and private enforcement efforts to deter auto theft, too much credit may be given to Lojack. However, the study does not find evidence that these other effects exist.

One last effect the study attempts to measure is the extent of the underprovision of an unobservable private security device. As mentioned above, if an individual's private benefit of purchasing a security device falls short of the social benefit, there may be a role for social intervention to encourage the purchasing of the device. The study estimates that the private benefits of Lojack are only about 10 percent of the social benefits of Lojack in terms of crime reduction. Thus, an individual may decide that it is not privately worth installing Lojack, especially given the fact that others may be installing the device, leading to an overall reduction in auto theft. If Lojack truly is an extremely efficient method for deterring auto theft, it may be in the authorities' best interest to provide incentives for more individuals to install the device. During the authors' sample period, one such incentive mechanism that was tried was allowing for state-mandated insurance discounts for car owners who installed Lojack. These discounts, however, appeared to be far below the level that would be considered socially optimal.

More guns, more or less crime

Compared to the Lojack example, a much widerspread private security device is a firearm. But firearms are also an offensive weapon. In approximately one-quarter of all violent crimes committed between the years 1993 and 2001, some kind of weapon was used by the offender. When a weapon was used, 37 percent of the time it was a firearm (usually a hand gun), 25 percent of the time a knife or sharp object, 16 percent of the time a blunt object, and 23 percent of the time another (or an unknown) weapon. When considering specific types of violent crimes, however, firearm use is seen to depend on the type of crime committed. For example, of all the homicides committed during the same sample years, firearms were used in 70 percent of them. For other violent crimes the use of firearms was less pronounced – 27 percent of the time for robberies, 8 percent of the time for assaults, and 3 percent of the time for rape (Bureau of Justice Statistics Special Report, *Weapon Use and Violent Crime*). Clearly, violent crime can be quite substantial with or without weapons, and with or without firearms, but the use of firearms (especially handguns) in the commission of violent crimes is often the starting point for the argument in favor of strict gun control laws. Ironically, it is also the starting point for the argument *against* strict gun control laws.

Since the 1990s there have been a number of studies that have examined the effects of gun control laws on crime. The main focus of these studies has been on laws that allow individuals to carry concealed handguns in public (known as "shall issue" laws). The main benefit of shall-issue laws is that, if more individuals are allowed to carry concealed handguns, criminals (even those who use weapons) may face higher costs of committing crimes such as murder, rape, aggravated assault, and robbery. To the extent that criminals are rational, these higher costs are predicted to reduce crime rates. The key point, however, is that the handguns must be *concealed*.

Consider, instead, a law that allows individuals to carry handguns, but only if clearly displayed on the body. Criminals in sizing up their potential victims, then, are likely to avoid tangling with obviously armed individuals and focus their efforts against easier prey. This is the diversion effect of private security measures discussed above. Crime will not be deterred, but simply diverted from the armed victim to the unarmed one. If individuals are allowed to carry concealed handguns, on the other hand, criminals will face a higher probability of *any* potential victim being armed. Not only do individuals who carry the weapons benefit, but so do other individuals. Just as seen in the case of the Lojack security device used to discourage car thieves, shall-issue laws have the ability to reduce the violent crime rate.

But the theoretical effects of shall-issue laws on the overall crime rate are ambiguous. Crime diversion across victims is only one kind of substitution criminals may consider. There is also the possibility that shall-issue laws will divert criminals from committing violent crimes toward committing nonviolent crimes. If more potential victims are carrying weapons, a criminal may decide that the costs of mugging someone are now too high, and decide instead to become a burglar or car thief. So, to evaluate the effects of shall-issue laws on the crime rate, it appears that the potential reduction in violent crimes must be weighed against the potential increase in nonviolent crimes. However, there are other factors to consider that suggest the violent crime rate may increase with the adoption of shall-issue laws.

First, the easier it is to secure a legal gun permit the easier it may be for criminals or potential criminals to get guns. Even with safeguards in place to restrict shall-issue permits, there may be dangerous individuals who will be able to satisfy whatever restrictions are in place. Second, individuals who are legally able to carry guns may decide to sell guns, or may have their guns stolen, by criminals who cannot get legal permits. Third, the more guns there are the more likely there will be gun-related accidents, suicides, and spontaneous acts of rage that turn deadly. Finally, to the extent that there are more armed potential victims, criminals may decide to escalate the use of violence themselves when committing crimes.

In 1997 an important study (Lott and Mustard, 1997) was published on the effect of shall-issue laws on the crime rate. The authors of the study attempt to address a simple question – Do shall-issue laws reduce or increase the crime rate? They reach an explicit conclusion:

> Our evidence implies that concealed handguns are the most cost-effective method of reducing crime thus far analyzed by economists, providing a higher return than increased law enforcement or incarceration, other private security devices, or social programs.
>
> (Lott and Mustard, 1997, p. 65)

They even claim that had the group of states that did not adopt shall-issue laws actually adopted them the policy change would have reduced victim costs in 1992 by $5.7 billion.

It is instructive, without going into too much detail, to delve deeper into how the $5.7 billion amount is calculated. The authors use their statistical model to predict the effect of shall-issue laws on several different crime rates. They then apply these predictions to the states that had not adopted the laws to answer a hypothetical question – How would crime be affected in these states had shall-issue laws been adopted? They then assign monetary values for the costs of each particular crime and calculate the net savings in victim costs.

Here are the numbers they use (Lott and Mustard, 1997, table 5, p. 29): there would have been 1,414 fewer murders (valued at $3 million per murder); 4,177 fewer rapes (valued at $90,000 per rape); 60,363 fewer aggravated assaults (valued at $23,000 per assault); 11,898 fewer robberies (valued at $8,000 per robbery); 191,743 more larcenies (valued at $380 per larceny); 89,928 more car thefts (valued at $3,800 per theft); and 1,052 more burglaries (valued at $1,500 per burglary). After totaling all the numbers, they wind up with a reduction in victim costs from violent crimes of $6.1 billion, an increase in victim costs from nonviolent crime of $400 million, for a net *reduction* in victim crime costs of $5.7 billion.

The authors also examine the costs and benefits of the *marginal* shall-issue permit. In other words, what are the costs and benefits of one additional concealed handgun permit? For example, the authors find that, in Pennsylvania, one additional shall-issue permit reduces the social cost of crime by $5,079. Much of this reduction ($4,986 of it) is due to the reduction in the murder rate brought about by concealed handguns. On the other hand, the private cost of gun ownership includes the purchase price of the gun and ammunition, permit filing fees, and (depending on the state) supervised training, but these costs on an annual basis typically are very small (such as under $50 for the Pennsylvania case). As found in the Lojack example, the authors conclude that there is an *under*investment in the purchase of guns because individuals who do not purchase guns can still benefit from the crime reduction brought about by *others* purchasing guns.

It should be made clear that these numbers need not be taken as fact. They are average numbers that can have quite a bit of variation around them. Furthermore, as always, there is substantial debate over the statistical methodology used in this study. But the numerical example is illustrative of a common technique economists use to quantify costs and benefits. It is simply a striking way of demonstrating that, when considering the trade-offs associated with shall-issue laws, this study concludes that the laws yield positive net benefits in crime reduction, and these net benefits may be large.

Or the net benefits may be negative. The above study initiated a small industry of follow-up studies that examined the same issue. Here is the strong conclusion of another study (Ayres and Donohue, 2003a) on shall-issue laws:

> There remains no robust, credible statistical evidence that the adoption of shall-issue laws will generally lower crime, and indeed the best, albeit

admittedly imperfect, statistical evidence presented thus far points in the opposite direction: that the adoption of shall-issue laws will generally increase crime.

If this sounds familiar, it is because the debate on shall-issue laws closely parallels that of the death penalty.

There is broad agreement that shall-issue laws have both the potential to reduce the crime rate through a deterrent effect, or increase the crime rate through an enhancement of violence effect. Economists expect that these two theoretical effects will trade off against each other, and therefore these offsetting effects must be sorted out empirically. In examining the empirical evidence, however, different studies reach completely different conclusions. Depending on the study, conclusions range from: the shall-issue laws reduce crime; they increase crime; or, they have no effect on crime. The differences in the studies are largely due to differences in data sets and to statistical methodological issues. And as with the studies on the deterrent effect of the death penalty, the authors of the gun control studies have passionate and sincere disagreements that are unlikely ever to be easily resolved.

One methodological issue in examining the effect of gun ownership on the crime rate is precisely how gun ownership is measured. Arguing that it is difficult for researchers to examine cross-state or cross-county gun ownership variations because the most reliable data are available only at the national level, one study (Duggan, 2001) proposes a proxy for gun ownership that allows for such regional variations. The author suggests that sales of the firearms magazine *Guns and Ammo* makes an excellent proxy for state and county gun ownership, and provides several justifications for the validity of this measure.

Most important, especially from a pragmatic standpoint, *Guns and Ammo* sales data are available at the state and county level. Also, the magazine places more emphasis on handguns (as opposed to long arms) when compared to other top-selling firearms magazines. Because handguns are common firearm weapons used in crimes and for self-defense, *Guns and Ammo* sales data may help identify handgun ownership patterns. The author also finds that *Guns and Ammo* sales are correlated with several individual characteristics (such as high school but not college graduate, living in southern or western states, and so on) that are themselves correlated with gun ownership. Furthermore, the author finds that *Guns and Ammo* regional sales are directly related to the death rate from gun accidents, the sale of firearms (measured by the number of gun shows), and National Rifle Association (NRA) membership. Taken together, *Guns and Ammo* sales can be a reasonable, but far from perfect, proxy for regional gun ownership.

Using the magazine sales as proxy, the main result of the study is that increases in gun ownership lead to significant increases in the overall homicide rate, but there is little relationship between gun ownership and other crime rates. The author is careful to rule out the reverse causation problem that gun ownership and homicides are positively related not because gun ownership leads to more homicides but because more homicides create a greater demand for gun ownership. Also, the author examines the effect of shall-issue laws on the crime rate and finds that these laws do not increase the rate of gun ownership and, in contrast to the finding of the earlier study discussed above, do not reduce the crime rate.

Here is another example of conflicting results in the gun control literature. Many states have adopted safe-storage laws for residential gun owners. These laws require gun owners to safely secure their guns within their homes. The most obvious benefit of these laws is that they make it more difficult for children to gain access to guns in the home. This can help prevent incidents such as when, on the last day of school in 2000, Nathaniel Brazill, a thirteen-year-old student in Florida, showed up with a handgun taken from an unlocked drawer of a family friend and murdered his teacher (*Economist*, November 23, 2002). Safe storage laws can also reduce the incidence of accidental shootings and teen suicides. On the other hand, to the extent that guns in the home offer protection against criminals, the possible lack of quick access to the guns may reduce the deterrent effect of gun ownership.

One study (Lott and Whitley, 2001) find that the safe-storage laws have little impact on accidental gun deaths or suicide rates, but have large *positive* effects on property and violent crime rates. They claim that during the five years after the passage of safe-storage laws, the fifteen states that adopted the law faced an annual average of 309 more murders, 3,860 more rapes, 24,650 more robberies, and 25,000 more aggravated assaults. Safe-storage laws, then, according to this study, greatly increase the crime rate, with no obvious offsetting benefits. But another study (Cook and Ludwig, 2002) finds that, whatever deterrent effect exists with residential gun ownership, it is more than offset by an increased burglary rate that is likely due to the attractiveness of guns as items burglars want to steal. They find that a 10 percent increase in gun ownership increases burglary rates by 3 percent to 7 percent. In a sense, then, it is possible to conclude that safe-storage laws may *reduce* burglaries if criminals feel that guns are not likely to be available to steal.

On the topic of juvenile access to guns, just as with adults such access can be argued to have two opposing effects. On the one hand, easy access to guns may increase the juvenile crime rate to the extent that the weapon facilitates criminal activity. On the other hand, easy access to guns may increase the juvenile's ability for self-protection against aggressors. If the aggregate data do not yield a significant relationship between gun possession and crime there may be two reasons: the enhanced crime effect and the self-protection effect perfectly offset each other; or, neither effect truly exists. One study (Mocan and Tekin, 2006) attempts to sidestep this problem by relying on individual-level data. More specifically, the authors have survey data from juveniles who are asked about the availability of guns at home. Over the course of the survey years, the variation in gun availability can be used to determine its effect on juvenile crime.

To isolate the effect of gun availability on crime, the authors are able to take advantage of an extremely rich data set that includes numerous other variables. Such variables include race, gender, age, height, weight, and perceived IQ of the juvenile, parents' education background, the availability of drugs or alcohol at home, religious background, and even the juvenile's degree of freedom at home (such as choosing own friends, amount of television watched, and deciding own curfew). After controlling for all these variables, the authors find that gun availability at home increases the juvenile's propensity to commit several types of crime (including robbery, burglary, theft and property damage). Furthermore, the availability of guns at home appears to have no effect on reducing the probability of the juvenile being a victim of crime. Thus, at least for the juveniles in this sample, the increased crime effect of gun availability is found to dominate the increased self-protection effect.

One possible social policy to deal with the easy access to guns problem is to strengthen the laws banning juvenile gun possession. This was done in 1994 with a federal law that banned possession of guns by individuals under the age of eighteen. At first blush, a law that bans juvenile gun possession may not be expected to have much of an effect on juvenile criminal behavior. After all, if it is already illegal for a juvenile to purchase or conceal a gun, how much more of an impact can making it illegal for a juvenile to *possess* a gun have on the individual's behavior? The potential impact can come from an increased sanction due an additional charge that can be placed upon a juvenile who purchases or conceals a weapon. Furthermore, it is technically possible for a juvenile to possess a gun without having concealed or purchased it. If, for example, a gun is found in a juvenile's bedroom or school locker, even if the gun was not purchased by the juvenile or carried outside, the possession of the weapon can lead to a charge. But one study (Marvell, 2001) finds that the bans appear to have no effect on reducing the juvenile crime rate, particularly the homicide rate.

Another gun control policy that has been used by the authorities is a gun buyback program. With buybacks, the authorities purchase guns from citizens who voluntarily turn them in. The obvious main goal of such a policy is to reduce the stock of guns and, as a result, hopefully reduce the amount of violent crime associated with gun use. Whether this goal of gun buybacks is realized, however, is an empirical issue. One study (Reuter and Mouzos, 2003) examines the effectiveness of a gun buyback program implemented in Australia during the late 1990s.

In April, 1996, a lone gunman killed thirty-five people in Port Arthur. In response to this tragic mass killing, the Australian federal and state governments rapidly initiated a number of new gun control policies. In order to own a firearm, an individual would be required to demonstrate a legitimate purpose and fitness of character, undertake safety training, and conform to safe storage requirements. Furthermore, certain classes of weapons were prohibited, such as self-loading rifles and shotguns. Finally, to promote the new controls, a large-scale gun buyback program was initiated. The buybacks were primarily for newly prohibited guns (especially long arms), but there was also an offer of amnesty (but no money) for individuals who handed in unlicensed firearms. The buybacks focused on long arms for two main reasons: they were the common weapon of choice in mass killings; and, handguns were already deemed to be tightly regulated.

By one measure – the number of guns turned in – the buyback program was quite successful. Although the numbers are rough approximations, the stock of firearms (prohibited and not prohibited) in Australia in 1996 was 3.2 million, and 650,000 (or about 20 percent) were turned in. Of the prohibited guns only, some estimates suggest that as much as 70 percent of that class of firearms were turned in. For the goal of reducing the stock of firearms in Australia, the buyback program was quite successful. For the goal of reducing the amount of crime associated with gun use, however, the buyback program appears to have been far less successful.

The authors find little or no evidence that the buyback program on its own reduced the crime rate. This is not a surprising result, given that the type of firearms targeted by the buyback program was not typically the weapon of choice for most types of violent crimes. The buyback program primarily focused on low-risk (with respect to crime) weapons such as long arms, as opposed to high-risk weapons such as handguns. On the other hand, the authors do suggest that, because there were no other mass killings with a firearm in a five-year period after the Port Arthur tragedy, it is possible that the new gun control policies reduced the incidence of the type of crime that motivated the new policies in the first place. But, overall, there simply may not have been enough time or enough data since the policy change to thoroughly assess its effect on the crime rate.

A brief mention should be made about the potential costs of the buyback program. The average buyback price paid per gun was approximately $500 (Australian). Total expenditures for buybacks, then, slightly exceeded $320 million (Australian). This expenditure, however, was not completely a *social* cost because money was transferred from the state to individuals who turned in their guns, but it certainly was an expense to the state. (Financing for the buyback program was provided by a 0.2 percent additional levy on national health insurance.) The most likely factor contributing to the social cost of the program was the administrative costs associated with promoting and implementing the gun buybacks. Whatever these costs were, possibly the best single lesson from the Australian example is that the administrative costs of buyback programs may yield their highest return if the buybacks focus on the type of weapons most associated with crime.

Whether gun control laws have an effect (in either direction) on the crime rate is undoubtedly an important question from a policy standpoint, but another more fundamental issue has to do with the fact that, to many, guns are just like any other consumer product – they are purchased because they are valued by consumers. Policy officials advocating gun bans may face displeased constituents, making gun bans politically unviable. For example, in Brazil in 2004, tough new gun control laws were enacted. Such controls included: stricter penalties for unregistered gun ownership; tighter control of gun ownership eligibility; raising the legal age of gun ownership from twenty-one to twenty-five; and, the opportunity for citizens to vote in a national referendum (the first of its kind in the world) to ban the sale of guns and ammunition outright (BBC News Americas, July 2, 2004). But this last attempt to enact an extreme gun control policy did not succeed, as Brazilians voted by a proportion of two to one to reject outright gun bans.

On a slightly different note, one interesting study (Glaeser and Glendon, 1998) concerning guns abstracts away from the relationship between guns and crime and instead asks a different question: Who owns guns? In a country where gun ownership is legal, it is not only criminals who own guns but also law-abiding citizens. Which law-abiding citizens own guns, and why? Does the demand for guns depend, at least in part, upon gun owners' lack of confidence or distrust in the government's ability to deter crime?

Using survey data from 1972 to 1994, the authors are able to distinguish between non-gun owners, individuals who own any type of gun (handguns, rifles, or shotguns), and individuals who only own handguns. They also use many of the common demographic and economic control variables such as age, gender, race, education, region of residence, income, and so on, to isolate their effects of interest that relate victimization and criminality to gun ownership. They first examine if gun ownership is related to the individual having been recently victimized, having been arrested (not for a traffic offense), and fearing crime in one's own neighborhood. They find no significant relationship between any of these variables and gun ownership in general, although fear of crime does increase handgun ownership. They also examine the relationship between gun ownership and the expectation of being a victim of crime in the future, or being arrested in the future, and find that these variables do not enhance gun ownership. They conclude that gun owners generally appear not to be criminals or victims.

Next, the authors try to account for gun ownership due to peer effects. They find that individuals who are surrounded by gun owners are more likely to be gun owners themselves, and this result is stronger for guns that are more difficult to conceal such as rifles and shotguns than it is for handguns. They also find that gun ownership appears to be positively related to individuals' taste for violent retribution, lack of confidence in the Supreme Court, belief that public officials don't care about them, and to the fewer police officers there are per square mile (in a state). These results support the idea that private and public crime deterrence may be *substitutes* for each other, a relationship I now consider in more detail.

Crime as a disease

Recently, economists have turned their attention to studying infectious diseases. This field of inquiry is known as *economic epidemiology*. According to medical dictionaries, epidemiology is defined as the study of populations in order to determine the frequency and distribution of disease, and to measure risks. For example, assume an infectious disease is spreading across the country. At any point in time, the population can be divided into two groups – those who have contracted the disease, and those who haven't. With this limited information, we can make a simple epidemiological prediction: the larger the fraction of infected people in the population, the larger the fraction of uninfected people who become infected in the future. Quite simply, the more people who have the disease the faster it will spread to the uninfected. This prediction often justifies rapid social intervention in fighting infectious diseases.

To an economist, however, the simple prediction is incomplete. It may very well be the case that the opposite occurs: the larger the fraction of infected people in the population, the *smaller* the fraction of uninfected people who become infected in the future. This is because individuals who have not yet been infected will have the incentive to take private precautions to prevent future infection, and the incentive to take these precautions will be *stronger* the larger the fraction of infected people in the population.

Consider a highly infectious disease such as AIDS. There may very well be a sound role for social intervention to prevent the spread of AIDS, possibly through education, or the subsidization of blood tests, or the subsidization of condom purchases, and so on. Yet private individuals will also take precautions to prevent the spread of the disease. An individual may reduce their number of sexual contacts, or be more careful in screening potential partners, or always use condoms. As the disease spreads, it is likely to be much better publicized, which in turn may lead to increased private precautions, which in turn will curtail the spread of the disease. To the extent that private individuals take precautions, the spread of the disease may be self-limiting even *without* social intervention. So what does all this have to do with rational crime analysis?

I am not claiming that crime can be spread in a manner similar to an infectious disease. The key link I want to make is the one between public expenditure on crime deterrence, and private expenditure. Just as with as with an infectious disease, as the crime rate increases it is likely that private individuals will take more precautions to deter crime. Conversely, as the crime rate decreases, individuals will take fewer precautions to deter crime. If the crime rate is affected by public expenditure on crime deterrence, then there is an indirect link between private and public expenditure.

For example, if the authorities devote more resources to fighting crime, such as by hiring more police officers or imposing lengthier prison sentences, the crime rate will be reduced. But this reduction in the crime rate will lead private individuals to devote fewer resources to crime deterrence, such as by purchasing fewer security devices, and this may lead to an *increase* in the crime rate. Thus, the original social goal of reducing the crime rate may be somewhat thwarted by its indirect effect (through the reduced crime rate) on private crime deterrence. It works the other way around also. If the authorities devote fewer resources to fighting crime, the crime rate will increase. This will lead private individuals to devote more resources to crime, and that may reduce the crime rate.

Notice that public expenditure and private expenditure are not directly linked, but instead are linked through the crime rate. As public expenditure affects the crime rate, the crime rate will affect the demand for private security measures. This is analogous to the rate of infection of a disease affecting the demand for private precautions. As the rate of infection increases, individuals not infected will increase their protective measures and help curtail the spread of the disease.

While there are not many empirical studies on the relationship between public and private expenditure on crime deterrence, there is some evidence that supports the existence of an indirect link between the two. One study (Philipson and Posner, 1996) finds that as the burglary crime rate increases there is a significant increase in the demand for burglar alarm systems – for every 100 burglaries per 100,000 population there is a 3 percent increase in the demand for alarm systems. They also find that when the burglary crime rate is held constant, there is no significant direct relationship between public expenditure and the demand for alarm systems. This evidence is consistent with their argument that public and private protection are related only through crime rates, and not directly. There is also an earlier study (Bartel, 1975) that examines how private businesses respond to crime rates, and it finds similar results. Firms' protection investments, such as hiring security guards, are strongly influenced by crime rates, but not directly by public expenditures.

The important public policy implication of this analysis is that public expenditure and private expenditure on crime deterrence are often *substitutes* for each other. This means that as public expenditure increases, private expenditure decreases, and as public expenditure decreases, private expenditure increases. Furthermore, because of the offsetting effect of public expenditure on private expenditure, there will be limits as to how high the crime rate can rise, as well as to how low the crime rate can fall, and the crime rate will tend to cycle. Private precautions tend to peak when the crime rate is high, and this helps limit the future growth of the crime rate. When the crime rate is low, private precautions tend to slack off, and this may allow the crime rate to rise again.

Crime rates and disease rates share another thing in common: both rates are almost impossible to *completely* eradicate. With roughly forty vaccines available, there still has been virtually no success in completely eradicating any infectious diseases. Substantial public effort to fight disease is often thwarted by the relaxed private effort that results from falling infection rates. This also holds true for the crime rate. Maybe, then, the best way to deter crime is to try to use only public expenditure or only private expenditure, so the two do not offset each other. But while the two expenditures may be substitutes for each other, they are not *perfect* substitutes.

It is unlikely that the efficient way to deter crime is only through public expenditure or only through private expenditure. On its own, public expenditure will be unable to deter all crime, not only because it is technically infeasible to do so, but also because it may not be desirable to do so. As discussed in Chapter 1, the resource cost of fighting crime can be prohibitive, and it will not likely be in society's best interest to devote an excessive amount of resources to try to eradicate crime. And, for identical reasons, private expenditure on its own will be unable to deter all crime. But in addition, as discussed above, many private precautions simply divert, as opposed to deter, crime. As with infectious diseases, the social goal of eliminating all crime is a noble one, but not a pragmatic one.

In conclusion, there are many trade-offs to consider when trying to determine optimal public policy to deter crime. The relationship between public and private expenditure adds another layer of complexity to the mix. Sound public policy must take into account the potential offsetting effects of private precautions. Yet there is still an additional complication. It is also possible that public and private expenditure *complement* each other, as in the Lojack example. Private individuals purchase the Lojack device, but that device is used to aid the *public* authorities in apprehending car thieves. The question of what role social policy should play, or *could* play for that matter, in either encouraging or discouraging private investment in security devices remains open, and intriguing.

Notes

For a discussion of private security measures as a crime deterrent or crime diversion, see the papers by Shavell (1991a), Hui-Wen and Ping (1994), and Ayres and Levitt (1998).

The economic literature on the relationship between gun control laws and the crime rate is extremely large. The paper by Lott and Mustard (1997) finding that right-to-carry laws are extremely effective at deterring crime is generally credited with sparking the modern debate. Other papers that are typically skeptical of the role of gun control laws in deterring crime are by Bronars and Lott (2001), Lott and Whitley (2001), Marvell (2001), Mustard (2001a), Plassmann and Whitley (2003), Moody and Marvell (2005), and Moorhouse and Wanner (2006). Papers that typically find support for the role of gun control laws in deterring crime are by Cook, Molliconi and Cole (1995), Cook and Leitzel, (1996), Alschuler (1997), Black and Nagin (1998), Dezhbakhsh and Rubin (1998), Ayres and Donohue (1999, 2003a, b), Duggan (2001), Cook and Ludwig (2002, 2004a, b, c, 2006), Rubin and Dezhbakhsh (2003), and Mocan and Tekin (2006).

Other papers on various aspects of the gun control debate are by Southwick (1997), Chaudhri and Geanakoplos (1998), Donohue and Levitt (1998), Glaeser and Glendon (1998), Bartley (1999) on gun rationing, Benson and Mast (2001), Helsey (2001) on stolen gun control, Lott (2001), Mullin (2001) and Reuter and Mouzos (2003) on gun buyback programs, Parker (2001), Cook and Leitzel (2002) on "smart" guns, Cook, Ludwig, Venkatesh and Braga (2005) on underground gun markets, Kwon and Baack (2005), and Mialon and Wiseman (2005).

The key paper on crime as a disease is by Philipson and Posner (1996), motivated by their earlier work (1993) on the economics of the AIDS epidemic. Other papers on the relationship between the private and public enforcement of law are by Bartel (1975), Landes and Posner (1975), Friedman (1979, 1984), Ben-Shahar and Harel (1995), Hakim, Rengert and Shachmurove (1995), Hay and Shleifer (1998), Witte and Witt (2001), Garoupa and Klerman (2002), and Helland and Tabarrok (2004).

7 Drugs and crime

Illicit drug use is quite common in the United States. In 2005, 112 million Americans age twelve or older reported illicit drug use at least once in their lifetime, 34 million reported drug use within the past year, and 19.5 million reported drug use within the past month (*2005 National Household Survey on Drug Use and Health*, September 2006). Of high school seniors in 2005, 44.8 percent reported ever having used marijuana or hashish, 8 percent ever having used cocaine, and 1.5 percent ever having used heroin (University of Michigan, *Monitoring the Future National Survey Results on Adolescent Drug Use: Overview of Key Findings 2005*, April 2006). Finally, in 2005 25 percent of all students in grades 9 through 12 reported someone had offered, sold, or given them an illegal drug on school property (Bureau of Justice Statistics and U.S. Department of Education, *Indicators of School Crime and Safety, 2006*, December 2006).

There is a strange dichotomy that exists when discussing illicit drugs. On the one hand, the authorities devote a substantial amount of resources to combat drug-related crimes. Recent estimates suggest that nearly 30 percent of all state and federal prisoners are imprisoned for a drug-related offense. The common language used by the authorities is that they are fighting a *war* on drugs. On the other hand, a large number of scholars and individuals argue in favor of drug *legalization*. From their perspective, no enforcement resources should be devoted to deterring what are currently considered drug-related crimes. In this chapter I attempt to account for this dichotomy.

Addiction and drug enforcement policy

A very common justification for keeping drugs illegal is that they are inherently dangerous, due to their addictive nature. Even if we are accepting of people who are willing to experiment with drugs only to satisfy their curiosity, their choice to quit may quickly be beyond their control. At first blush, then, it seems to make good sense to protect individuals from being overwhelmed by addictive products. But, to an economist, an important question remains: Is it possible that individuals *willingly* choose to become addicted to certain goods?

The Merriam Webster online dictionary broadly defines the word addiction to mean "persistent compulsive use of a substance known by the user to be harmful."

This succinct definition creates an immediate paradox. If the user *knows* that a substance is harmful, why use it in the first place? Maybe the user doesn't realize the harmful nature of the substance until it is too late, or perhaps there is an alternative explanation. Just as with any rational criminal, the potential drug user can weigh the costs and benefits of using an addictive substance and choose to consume the product if the benefits exceed the costs. Economists refer to this as *rational addiction*. But is this an oxymoron? Can an addict ever be rational?

It is a fairly common belief that addiction implies irrationality. But the concept of rational addiction is actually quite intuitively pleasing. A rational addict's choice to consume a product today depends primarily on two things: how much of the product was consumed in the past, and how much of the product will be consumed in the future. In other words, the key concept behind rational addiction is considering how consumption of the product is linked across time for the addict.

For example, assume I was a smoker who smoked five cigarettes a day up until a year ago, when I had to confront an overly stressful event in my life. To handle the stress, I increased my smoking to ten cigarettes a day. Since then, I have put that stressful event behind me, yet I have continued smoking ten cigarettes a day. What this story tells us is that because the stressful event increased my past consumption of smoking, it also increased my current consumption. As another example, assume the government announces a tax increase on cigarettes that will take place in a year from now. As a rational addict, I know the tax hike will reduce my future consumption of cigarettes and, as a result, I decide to reduce my current consumption as well.

What these examples illustrate is that past, current, and future consumption all *complement* each other. An increase in past or future consumption leads to an increase in current consumption. The converse is also true – a decrease in past or future consumption leads to a decrease in current consumption. When consumption in one period directly affects consumption in another period, this is known as the *reinforcement effect*. In the rational addiction framework, a product is defined to be addictive if it exhibits a reinforcement effect. Notice that this is a very general definition. We don't have to debate whether a substance is physically addictive, psychologically addictive, or some combination of the two. A product is addictive if current consumption affects future consumption, and this can be true for a wide variety of activities such as exercising, reading, shopping, playing video games, listening to music, and so on.

The single most important implication of the rational addiction model is that addicts are not "trapped" by an addictive product. Instead, they make informed, conscious decisions to consume a product with the knowledge that current consumption in and of itself will affect future consumption. Rational addicts consider their lifetime horizons when making consumption decisions. This counters the view that addicts are irrationally myopic, trading off their future well-being for immediate gratification. Rational addicts may very well be sacrificing their future health by consuming addictive substances today, but it is done knowingly.

Another implication of rational addiction is that addicts can adjust their consumption levels based on current and future changes in their environment. The belief that addicts must consume a certain amount of a product, no matter what, is not the case. Rational addicts can respond to changes in price, income, information, costs of quitting, and so on. Understanding how sensitive addicts are to these variables is crucial in evaluating the impact of policies aimed at reducing the consumption of addictive products. If the goal of increased punishment is to reduce the incidence of illicit drug use, will that be an effective policy? If so, how effective?

Justifying social intervention to protect rational addicts from themselves is problematic. By definition, rational addicts optimize over their entire lifetime. They have a full understanding of the costs and benefits of their behavior, and they choose to consume addictive products when the benefits exceed the costs. Also, it is reasonable to anticipate that rational addicts can unilaterally change their behavior over time. For example, a rational addict, when young, may decide to consume drugs because at that time in their life the health costs are modest, but choose to quit when older and facing more severe health costs. In short, because rational addicts are not harming themselves, there is little justification for social policy to protect them.

A better justification exists to protect addicts who are not behaving rationally in the sense that they lack the information to make well informed decisions. Perhaps some addicts have poor access to information, or even with access they lack the ability to accurately understand it. Individuals who have poor information may be making the best decisions they can, *given* the information they have, but these decisions are not optimal relative to those made in a world of perfect information. The difficult question here is whether to intervene by directly controlling drug use through the enforcement of laws, or to provide the information to the individuals so that they can make better decisions. Notice that, in the latter instance, the social objective may not be to reduce drug use but to encourage *optimal* drug use. For example, individuals who *overestimate* the risks of drug use and become more accurately informed may choose to *increase* their drug use. Encouraging optimal drug use, whether that decreases or increases drug use, fits neatly into the realm of the rational addiction framework.

While it may seem that there is little justification to control the behavior of fully informed rational addicts, new research adds an interesting twist to the story. Consider two individuals who are fully informed about the benefits and costs of becoming drug users. Both individuals realize that they are trading off current benefits for future health costs. One key difference between the two individuals may be in how they weigh future events over current events. The individual who is less concerned about the future (that is, the individual who is more myopic) will be more likely to become a drug user. Thus, the rational addiction model predicts that shortsighted, or present-oriented, individuals are more likely to become addicts compared to those who place more value on their future well-being. The individual who chooses to become an addict does not regret that decision, now or later. Likewise, the individual who does not become an addict does not regret that decision, now or later. But what about the real-world possibility of an individual who ends up regretting a current decision?

For example, assume that today I am making the decision to become a heroin addict. As part of this decision, I consider the costs of quitting in the future and come to the conclusion that I will become an addict today because of the reasonable costs of quitting in five years from now. When the five years are up, I actually do quit. But now let's assume that you are considering the same decision that I am based on the same information. You too decide to become an addict today because of your belief that you will quit in five years. Unfortunately, when the five years are up, *at that time* you decide not to quit. In economic jargon, my decision to quit is *time-consistent* – I followed through with what I thought I was going to do right from the beginning. Your decision is *time-inconsistent* – you became an addict because of your intention to quit, but then you didn't follow through. You actually may end up regretting your decision to consume heroin in the first place, but I experience no such regret.

This form of time inconsistency is caused by the specific nature of an individual's shortsightedness. When, from today's perspective, you look ahead at two *future* periods, you may not be very myopic about the second period relative to the first one. But when you actually arrive at the first future period, at that time you may be very myopic about the next period. In other words, how you trade-off future costs and benefits from today's perspective may not be how you trade-off the same costs and benefits when the future arrives. If this type of myopia leads addicts to eventually regret their current decisions, social intervention may be justified to protect addicts from themselves. Actually, with time-inconsistency, addicts may *welcome* social intervention to control their behavior if they recognize their self-control problem. If you plan on becoming a drug user today because you are relying on your intention to quit in the future, *and* you realize that you may end up not being able to quit when the time comes, you may appreciate social policy to help discourage your current drug use.

We can now put all of the above discussion together and consider the justifications for social policy to control drug use to protect addicts from themselves. The strongest justification is for addicts who understand that they have self-control problems or realize they are not able to make well informed decisions. Because the social control is demanded by the drug users, it must be improving their welfare. The weakest justification is for rational addicts. These individuals fully understand the costs and benefits of drug use, they don't have self-control problems, and they don't welcome social control of their behavior. Such control, then, lowers their welfare. Finally, there are those addicts who don't realize they have self-control problems, or don't realize that they are poorly informed about the true costs and benefits of their actions. Traditionally, these individuals are thought of as providing a strong rationale for social control. After all, isn't the role of paternalistic policies to protect people from themselves precisely because they don't truly appreciate that they are harming themselves? Unfortunately, it may not be that simple.

If addicts do not recognize their self-control or lack of information problems, they do not appreciate that they are making poor decisions relative to some other state of the world. As such, they do not appreciate social control of their behavior. Any such control, then, will be perceived by the addicts as lowering their welfare. If it is these individuals' welfare that is being counted as *social* welfare, social welfare does not increase as they are protected. Some may argue that these individuals' welfare is increasing even if they don't perceive it to be, but this raises a tricky question: Can someone be made better-off without realizing it? If you believe the answer is no, you may not support paternalistic social policies that are never appreciated by the individuals they are aimed at. If you believe the answer is yes, you may support paternalistic policies that protect these individuals from themselves.

The main point I want to make is that it can be difficult justifying social control of addictive substances to protect individuals from themselves. Such justification is not completely without merit, but economic reasoning can be used to challenge the belief that addiction is necessarily bad. There are, however, other justifications for controlling drug use that fit more neatly into the economics of crime framework. Because drug users and suppliers may impose substantial costs on *others*, social policy may be used to protect victims from criminals.

Externals costs of illicit drug use

It is a common belief that drug users often steal to support their habits. In 2004, 17 percent of state prisoners and 18 percent of federal prisoners said they committed their current offense to obtain money for drugs. Furthermore, 32 percent of state prisoners and 26 percent of federal prisoners said they committed their current offense while under the influence of drugs (Bureau of Justice Statistics, *Drug Use and Dependence, State and Federal Prisoners, 2004*). But even if it were the case that all individuals who commit property crimes use drugs, that doesn't tell us much about what percentage of drug users commit property crimes. Thus, there is a question about the extent of criminal acts committed by drug users. Furthermore, there is also a question about the direction of the causation between drug use and property crime. Is it that drug users become thieves only to support their drug habits, or are individuals who have a propensity to become thieves also likely to have a propensity to become drug users? If the latter is true, policies to discourage drug use may have little effect on discouraging property crime.

Let's assume that it is true that increased drug use leads to increased property crime. Using this fact to *justify* drug control policies may be ironic if it is the policies in and of themselves that *explain* the fact. For example, if increased drug control enforcement makes it more costly for drug users to obtain drugs, especially if the control raises the monetary price of drugs, it is possible that drug users will commit more property crimes to support their more expensive habits. On the other hand, if there is a physical and psychological relationship between drug use and property crime (such as drug users commit property crimes because the drugs make them more aggressive or less inhibited), social control policies to limit drug use may indeed lower property crime.

Another common justification for drug control policy is that it can discourage drug use that lowers the productivity of workers. If the detrimental physical and psychological effects of drug use make workers less productive, either while they are on the job or because they are frequently absent from work, there may be spillover effects that affect not only individual firms but the economy as a whole. And, to the extent that drug use leads to unemployment, further social costs may be borne. There is a fairly large body of empirical research that addresses these issues but, as usual, the results are mixed.

While it is difficult to directly measure workers' productivity, economists use wages as a proxy for productivity. The basic idea is that more productive workers earn higher wages than do less productive workers. If drug use lowers productivity, we expect drug users to earn lower wages than do non-drug users. But the causation may also work the other way. If workers who earn more tend to buy more drugs than do workers who earn less, we may observe a positive relationship between drug use and wages. Thus, researchers must be careful to separate out the two possible connections between drug use and wages. Even with being careful, the available evidence is not conclusive that drug users earn significantly lower wages compared to non-drug users. Two studies (Gill and Michaels, 1992; Kaestner, 1991) actually find that drug use *increases* wages. One possible explanation for this result is that, just as a worker with a headache may be more productive when taking aspirin, a drug user may rely on an illicit substance to "make it through the day." Ultimately, however, the difficulties in linking drug use to worker productivity involve methodological issues in the empirical research.

In a thorough series of studies (MacDonald and Pudney, 2000a, b, 2001), the authors use data from the 1994 and 1996 British Crime Survey (BCS) to examine the relationship between drug use and labor market outcomes such as unemployment and worker productivity. Although the BCS does not provide individual wage information, it does provide information on occupational classes, ranging from the professional/managerial class through the skilled, partly skilled, and unskilled classes. (There is also a much more narrow listing of 899 individual occupations the authors sometimes use.) Thus, instead of using wages as a proxy for worker productivity, the authors use *occupational attainment* as a proxy instead. Also included in the BCS are specific questions about the respondent's use of commonly abused drugs: had they ever taken the drug; had they taken the drug in the past twelve months; had they taken the drug in the past month? The data these questions provide allow the authors to distinguish between past and fairly current drug use and their effect on labor market outcomes.

Although there are differences in what the authors examine in each study, some common results emerge. The authors' key findings are that past drug use significantly increases the probability of current unemployment, but there appears to be little evidence of a relationship between drug use and worker productivity (as measured by occupational attainment). The authors conclude that public policy should be focused mainly on the unemployment effect of drug use, rather than its effect on the productivity of workers.

Another important lesson from these and other studies (French, Roebuck and Alexandre, 2001; Kaestner and Grossman, 1998) is that defining a worker simply as a "drug user" may be misleading – differences between drug users need to be taken into account. For example, recreational drug users tend to have fewer adverse employment effects compared to heavy drug users. Younger workers who have not consumed drugs for many years appear to suffer fewer adverse effects compared to older workers who have consumed drugs for a longer period of time. Finally, there also may be differences between male and female drug users. These differences in the personal characteristics of drug users make it that much more difficult to identify effective drug control policies.

Drug control policy can be justified by pointing to several other potential costs of drug use. If drug users suffer frequent health problems, they may impose costs upon the health care system that are borne by others, either through increased premiums in private insurance pools or through social insurance programs like Medicaid. Drug use can also lead to an overburdening of emergency room care. For example, in 2005, the Drug Abuse Warning Network (DAWN) estimated that nearly 1.4 million emergency department visits in the United States were associated with drug misuse or abuse. Approximately 450,000 visits involved cocaine use, 240,000 visits involved marijuana use, 165,000 visits involved heroin use, 140,000 visits involved stimulant use, and other drugs such as PCP or ecstasy were much less frequently involved (U.S. Department of Health and Human Services, *Drug Abuse Warning Network, 2005: National Estimates of Drug-related Emergency Department Visits*, 2007). Another peculiar health cost of drug use involves severe tooth decay caused by smoking the acidic drug methamphetamine. A report to the American Dental Association in 2005 emphasized that authorities have estimated that more than 15 percent of the nation's prisoners suffer from this form of tooth decay, imposing substantial dental costs on the prison system (Cleveland *Plain Dealer*, February 11, 2006).

Another concern is that drug users may drive while under the influence, thus imposing direct costs upon themselves and others through increased accident rates. A study of automobile drivers in Auckland, New Zealand (Blows *et al.*, 2005), finds that habitual marijuana use by drivers (defined as marijuana use at least once a week over the past twelve months) leads to a tenfold increase in the risk of a car crash injury. Finally, other potential social costs may be incurred by family members and friends who bear resource and emotional costs when dealing with drug users. Even individuals who have no personal connections to drug users may bear psychological costs associated with the knowledge that some members of society appear to be suffering from drug use.

A 1992 study (jointly published by the National Institute on Drug Abuse and the National Institute on Alcoholism and Alcohol Abuse) estimates the total economic costs of drug abuse in the United States for that year to be approximately $97 billion. A breakdown of the total costs shows $10 billion are due to health care expenditures; $69 billion due to worker productivity losses (attributed to lost earnings of drug users due to premature death, illness, imprisonment, and lost earnings to victims of drug-related crimes); and, $18 billion due to governmental expenditures toward the criminal justice and social welfare systems. (For a summary of the study see Cartwright, 1999.) Whether direct or indirect, real or emotional, the social costs of drug use appear to be substantial. But that still leaves us with the next important question: How effective are drug control policies in dealing with the drug problem?

Drug enforcement policies

The primary goal of drug control policy is to reduce the consumption of drugs. One way in which to achieve this goal is to enforce supply-side controls that make it more costly for drug producers to produce and distribute their product. Such controls may involve increases in the expected punishment drug producers face, either by devoting more resources to apprehension and conviction, or by enhancing the severity of punishment. The authorities may also more directly control the supply of drugs by destroying drug crops before they are harvested, or by seizing drugs somewhere along the line of distribution before they reach the final consumer. For example, in March, 2007, U.S. Border Patrol Agents seized nearly 3,000 pounds of marijuana (worth $2 million) when they stopped and searched a pick-up truck entering the country (*Desert Sun*, March 20, 2007). Whatever supply-side controls are chosen, the belief is that these restrictions will increase the costs of producing drugs and ultimately raise the price of drugs to users. With a higher price, we expect consumption to decline. But exactly how much of a change in drug consumption can authorities expect their policies to create?

If addicts are "trapped" by their addiction, it is common to believe that modest price changes will have little effect on consumption. But, as argued above, to the extent that addicts are rational, they may respond in predictable ways to changes in price, income, information, and so on. While it is well accepted that consumption and price are inversely related – the higher the price, the lower the consumption – the key question is: How *sensitive* is drug consumption to increases in price? To an economist, this question can be reworded as: What is an illicit drug's *elasticity of demand*?

The elasticity of demand directly measures the sensitivity of consumption to price. For example, assume that a drug's price increases by 5 percent. We expect to observe a reduction in consumption, but will that reduction be greater than 5 percent or less than 5 percent? (The reduction may also be exactly 5 percent, but I'm going to ignore this possibility for ease of discussion.) If the reduction in consumption is greater than 5 percent, we say that the demand for the drug is *elastic*. This means, a small percentage price change leads to a larger percentage consumption change. If the reduction in consumption is less than 5 percent, we say that the demand for the drug is *inelastic*. This means, a small percentage price change leads to an even smaller percentage consumption change.

To further elaborate, if price increases by 5 percent, assume that consumption falls by 10 percent. This implies that the consumption effect is twice the price effect, or the elasticity of demand is –2.0. (The minus sign represents the inverse relationship between price and consumption.) If consumption were to fall by only 2.5 percent, this implies that the consumption effect is half the price effect, or the elasticity of demand is –0.5. When the elasticity of demand is less than –1 (such as –2.0), the demand is elastic. When the elasticity of demand is between –1 and 0 (such as –0.5), the demand is inelastic. Controlling drug use, then, will be easier to do the more sensitive consumption is to price. So, what are the elasticities of demand for some of the most common drugs?

Although it is difficult to achieve a high degree of precision when estimating elasticities of demand for real-world products, especially illicit products, there is a body of evidence that provides useful ranges (see the surveys by Caulkins and Reuter, 1998, and MacDonald, 2004). Some of the studies estimating the elasticity of demand for heroin have found numbers between –0.25 and –1.80. For cocaine, numbers have been reported between –0.72 and –2.51. And for marijuana, typical numbers fall between –0.36 and –1.51. Thus, for each drug, the sensitivity of consumption to price ranges from being inelastic to being elastic.

In evaluating drug control polices to reduce consumption, it is encouraging that the evidence suggests drug users are indeed sensitive to price, at least to some extent. But it may be crucial to distinguish between elastic demand responses and inelastic demand responses. Certainly, the more sensitive consumption is to price the greater reduction in consumption these polices may induce. Reduced consumption, however, may not be the only concern. We may also want to consider how the drug control policies affect consumer *spending*.

If it is true that some drug users support their habit by committing property crimes, how much these users spend on drugs is important information. Just because a policy reduces the consumption of drugs, that doesn't necessarily imply that spending will also be reduced. If the demand is inelastic, a 5 percent price increase may reduce consumption by 2.5 percent, but it will lead to an *increase* in spending because the increased price effect outweighs the reduced consumption effect. And more spending may very well lead to more property crime. If demand is elastic, on the other hand, the price increase will lead to reduced consumption *and* reduced spending, possibly a more desirable outcome from a social perspective.

Another avenue for drug enforcement control policies to pursue is through the demand side of the market. Demand-side policies include increasing the expected punishment to drug users through changes in the certainty and/or severity of punishment, encouraging or subsidizing treatment for users, providing information about the harmful effects of drug use, and so on. For example, the "Montana Meth Project" presents advertisements aimed at keeping teens away from methamphetamine. One such television ad begins with a teen calmly saying, "I'm really close with my mom. I always have been." Then the mother says to the teen, who is going through her purse, "What are you doing?" The teen angrily responds, "Nothing. Leave me alone. Just shut up." Then the teen hits his mother.

As with supply-side policies, the goal of demand-side policies is to reduce consumption, but this is done by reducing the demand for drugs *at every price*. What this means is that, whatever amount an individual would consume at a given price before any control polices are in effect, after the control takes hold the individual will consume less even if the price doesn't change. It is not likely, however, that price won't change. Demand-side controls tend to lower the price by reducing how much users are willing to pay for drugs.

In general, supply-side controls tend to reduce consumption and increase the price of drugs. Demand side controls also tend to reduce consumption, but usually reduce the price of drugs. Because both types of policies are often used simultaneously, the prediction is that successful drug enforcement policy reduces consumption of drugs, but has an indeterminate effect on price. Thus, the usual goal of drug enforcement policies – reduced consumption of drugs – is typically expected. But in achieving its goal, how costly is drug enforcement policy?

The costs of drug enforcement policies

There is ample evidence that the war on drugs is a costly war to maintain. For example, President George W. Bush's 2007 federal budget proposed an allocation of $12.7 billion for reducing illegal drug use in the United States. The funding was divided into three key priorities. Approximately $1.7 billion was allocated to Priority I, "Stopping use before it starts: Education and community action." This includes funding for such programs as student drug testing, research grant assistance to local educational agencies, antidrug media campaigns, and so on. Approximately $2.5 billion is allocated to Priority II, "Intervening and healing America's drug users." This includes funding for such programs as new ways to treat methamphetamine addiction, substance abuse and mental health services, and so on. Finally, approximately $8.5 billion is allocated to Priority III, "Disrupting the market." This includes funding for such programs as Afghanistan counterdrug support, customs and border protection, community-oriented policing services, and so on (Office of National Drug Control Policy, *National Drug Control Strategy, FY 2007 Budget Summary*).

But not only must we consider the resources that are used to fight the war, it is likely that the war itself enhances the level of violence associated with the production of drugs. While the main goal of prohibition is to eliminate the drug trade, the actual effect of prohibition is to drive the trade underground. Producers in an underground industry do not get to rely on the court system to resolve business disputes. If there is a conflict between suppliers, or between customers and suppliers, the contentious parties cannot hire lawyers to resolve their problems. Even if explicit contracts are agreed upon, these contracts have no legal standing. Thus, dispute resolution in an underground industry typically involves violence. But one must be careful to note that drug use itself may lead to increased violence or crime by users, and if prohibition reduces the consumption of drugs, it may also reduce the level of user violence. In all, then, the relationship between prohibition and violence in drug markets is, in theory, ambiguous.

One interesting empirical study (Miron, 1999) attempts to provide empirical verification of the direct relationship between drug prohibition and violence in the United States throughout most of the twentieth century. The study incorporates three ideas. First, because drugs are prohibited, violence in the drug industry serves the purpose of dispute resolution. Second, the *degree* of prohibition at any point in time affects the degree of violence at that point in time. Finally, the degree of prohibition at a point in time can be measured by the degree of enforcement expenditure at that point in time. The basic premise of the study is that it offers a distinction between *prohibiting* the sale and use of a drug versus *enforcing* that prohibition.

Making it illegal to consume a specific drug is one thing, but enforcing the law is something else entirely. If enforcement expenditures increase because the authorities have to resort to more violent means to apprehend dangerous drug suppliers, this in turn may lead the drug suppliers to resort to more violence in order to avoid apprehension. Also, if increased enforcement is effective in removing certain suppliers from the market, other suppliers may resort to violence in competing for the now vacant positions. Along with some more subtle reasons, simply put, the more expenditures devoted to prohibition the more violence we expect to see.

In testing this hypothesis, the study examines how the U.S. homicide rate throughout the twentieth century was affected by the degree of enforcement of drug control laws. To isolate the impact of the enforcement of the laws, the study is able to control for other important factors that are expected to affect the homicide rate. These control variables include deterrent factors such as the incarceration rate and the use of the death penalty, economic conditions such as the unemployment rate and per capita income, demographic factors such as the age composition of the population, and, finally, the availability of guns. The main empirical result found is that the homicide rate is 25 percent to 75 percent higher than it would have been had there been no prohibition of drugs. As is always the case, how much we can rely on the empirical results of any single study is questionable, but the idea behind the study suggests that there may be a serious down side to drug prohibition.

Another problem with drug enforcement policy involves its effectiveness. The war on drugs is not only a costly war to fight, it is also a difficult one. On the supply side, if the authorities increase the pressure against one specific country's export of drugs to the United States, there is always another country ready to fill in the gap. Destroy one crop of drugs, another crop can be planted. Make it more difficult to produce one type of drug, another type of drug can readily take its place. Arrest street dealers, others are ready to step into their place. On the demand side, the probability of apprehension appears to be small, possibly explaining why so many individuals at least experiment with drugs.

With every dollar devoted to drug control polices there is one dollar less devoted to other crime deterrence policies. It is possible, then, that the war on drugs "causes" increases in other types of crimes. For example, as discussed above, if drug users tend to commit property crimes to support their habits, restricting the use of drugs through either supply-side or demand-side policies is believed to be an effective way to reduce property crime. But if enforcement resources are drawn away from directly fighting property crime to combat drug use, it may be the case that property crime increases because of a weakening of the deterrent effect. One study examining property crime in the state of Florida (Benson, Kim, Rasmussen and Zuehlke, 1992) concludes that increased property crime is at least partially the result of increased drug enforcement policies. Other studies (Brumm and Cloninger, 1995; Benson and Rasmussen, 1998) find that violent crime rates are also positively related to increased drug enforcement.

Furthermore, as more individuals are imprisoned due to drug-related crimes, it is possible that other types of criminals may be "crowded out" of prison. This crowding-out effect may increase other types of crimes through a reduction in the deterrent and incapacitation effects of prison. One empirical study, however, (Kuziemko and Levitt, 2004) finds that while a crowding-out effect does exist, the overall effect of incarcerating drug offenders does lead to a small reduction in property and violent crimes. But the study also concludes that these small benefits of fighting the war on drugs are unlikely to outweigh the substantial enforcement costs.

When putting together the costs and benefits of drug prohibition, many economists conclude that a strong case can be made for the legalization of drugs. I believe the call for legalization stems from two considerations. First, to the extent that drug users are rational and understand the nature of their consumption patterns, the benefits of drug prohibition may be overstated. By and large, the concept of paternalism is a tough sell to many economists. And even though there is a resurgence of economic thinking emphasizing the role of control policies for drug users who may not be fully rational, the "victimless crime" aspect of drug use is often asserted. Second, and more important, the drug war is extremely costly to maintain and of questionable effectiveness. Even if drug users and suppliers impose substantial costs on society, it is possible that many of these costs are a result of the prohibition itself.

Legalization, it is argued, may be preferred to prohibition because of the vast enforcement costs saving that will be realized. There will be no more need to apprehend, convict, and punish drug-related criminals. These resources can now be put to use either elsewhere in the criminal justice system, or to some other use entirely. Furthermore, legalization can also eliminate whatever costs are attributed to prohibition itself (such as increased violent and property crime). The down side of legalization, however, is that it is likely to increase drug use, possibly even greatly increase drug use. To whatever extent drug use is costly either to the user or to others, legalization will exacerbate those costs.

To compensate for the increase in drug use, proponents of drug legalization look to the cigarette and alcohol markets as examples of how to legalize and control certain products. To restrict legal drug use, control policies such as taxation, drug education, and the encouragement or subsidization of treatment may be used. To protect minors, age restriction polices can be enacted and enforced. Alternatively, drugs can be made legally available through prescription only. Up until the late 1950s, heroin was a legally prescribed drug in Great Britain, and there appeared to be little concern of heroin addiction as a serious social problem. In fact, in 1955 there were fewer than fifty heroin addicts in the whole of Britain, although there were many more casual users of the drug. Today in Britain, heroin is legally prescribed by a limited number of doctors to a small group of patients who are fighting addiction to the drug (*BBC News Magazine*, January 25, 2006). Yet even if legalization does lead to increased drug use compared to prohibition, it is still possible that the costs of legalization will fall short of the costs of prohibition.

Another aspect of the legalization argument that is often discussed is the different policy stances that may be applied to "soft" drugs (most commonly cannabis, but also amphetamines, mushrooms, amyl nitrate, and so on), versus "hard" drugs (such as heroin, crack, cocaine, and methadone). While some argue for drug legalization across the board, a more moderate view is for legalization (or at least a more relaxed policy stance) for soft drugs. But even if soft drug use is, in and of itself, not as socially costly an activity as is hard drug use, a common argument against the legalization of soft drugs involves the *gateway effect* – the tendency for soft drug use to lead to subsequent hard drug use and criminal activity.

One study (Pudney, 2003) uses British data to examine the gateway effect. The author cites some (very crude) evidence concerning the extent of drug use in the United Kingdom. In the late 1990s, roughly £7 billion (or approximately £2.20 per person per week) was spent on drugs, with about two-thirds of that expenditure devoted to heroin, crack, and cocaine. Estimates of the social costs of drug use range between £11 billion and £19 billion, and include costs to the National Health Service, the criminal justice system, the social benefits system, and to the victims of drug-related crimes. Nearly all of these costs are attributable to drug users with serious uncontrolled dependencies. Thus, if there is a gateway effect, soft drug use may ultimately lead to substantial social costs, strengthening the argument against legalization of such drugs.

The author's data are drawn from the British 1998 Youth Lifestyles Survey, covering the twelve-to-thirty age group of approximately 3,900 respondents. The survey provides information (for various age groups) on current and past behavior, and current and past family circumstances. The crucial information for the author's approach is the onset ages for different drugs (earlier for soft drugs, later for hard drugs), and the onset ages for different crimes (earlier for minor crimes, later for serious crimes). At first blush, then, it appears that there is a simple age progression from soft drug use and minor crimes to hard drug use and more serious crimes. But this progression does not imply that soft drug use *causes* hard drug use and serious criminal behavior.

The author's results (using a fairly sophisticated empirical approach) suggest that hard drug use and serious criminal behavior are not caused by soft drug use. Instead, such behaviors are more responsive to social and family factors (poverty, single-parent household, strong drug culture in terms of percent of drug users in the population, and so on). The study concludes by suggesting that, even if a policy directed at reducing soft drug use could be effective, that particular policy would have little impact on reducing the substantial social costs associated with hard drug use and serious crimes. In other words, this one study does not find empirical support for the gateway effect.

Because there are a number of economists who believe that drug enforcement policy is costly and largely ineffective, they often raise a simple question: Why do these policies continue to be implemented? One obvious answer is that there are many people who feel that drug use is bad, period. To this group, drugs are a blight on society and they are worth fighting against, even at tremendous costs. I have no doubt that this argument holds true to some extent. But some scholars believe a seemingly more cynical answer is correct – there are public officials who have much to gain from drug enforcement policies.

In Chapter 2 I discussed one of the problems of using fines as a punishment. If the authorities keep the revenue generated by the monetary sanctions, they have an incentive to overdeter certain crimes. Many states have asset seizure laws as part of their drug enforcement polices. These laws allow at least a portion of the seized assets to go to the authorities making the seizure, as well as additional portions going into general or specific public funds. For example, in March, 2005, a Pontoon Beach (Illinois) police officer seized $3.3 million in a drug-related arrest. Of the total amount, the Pontoon Beach police department kept $2.37 million, the Federal Drug Enforcement Agency asset forfeiture fund kept $658,000, and the Madison County state's attorney office kept $263,555 (*Belleville News – Democrat*, March 16, 2006). The benefit of the seizure laws is that they impose additional punishment on criminals and, therefore, may create an added deterrent effect. But these laws may also affect how the authorities use resources to fight drug crimes.

One study (Mast, Benson and Rasmussen, 2000) examines the effect of asset seizure laws on the extent of police drug enforcement effort. They find that in jurisdictions where police are allowed to keep a portion of the assets, there is a significant increase in drug arrests (controlling for several other factors that affect police drug enforcement effort). While more drug arrests may appear to be evidence of effective drug enforcement, as discussed above it may also represent an inefficient use of resources. If resources are being drawn away from other criminal deterrence efforts, or from other drug-related efforts (such as treatment programs), only because the police profit from drug-related asset seizures, the laws themselves are providing poor incentives for the authorities to consider the efficient use of resources from a *social* perspective. Thus, even if drug legalization is not the best social policy to pursue, the study concludes that reforms in the current drug enforcement policies may be needed.

Notes

Papers on rational addiction, drug prices, and topics relating to controlling individual drug use are by Becker and Murphy (1988), Caulkins (1995), Caulkins and Reuter (1996, 1998), Grossman, Chaloupka and Anderson (1998), Grossman and Chaloupka (1998), Rasmussen, Benson and Mocan (1998), Mocan and Corman (1998), Camerer, Issacharoff, Loewenstein, O'Donoghue and Rabin (2003), and Thaler and Sunstein (2003). Two excellent survey papers are by Messinis (1999) and MacDonald (2004).

There is a large literature on drug use and its effect on labor market outcomes such as productivity and employment. Representative papers of this literature are by Kaestner (1991, 1994a, b, 1998), Gill and Michaels (1992), Buchmueller and Zuvekas (1998), Burgess and

Propper (1998), Kaestner and Grossman (1998), MacDonald and Pudney (2000a, b, 2001), and French, Roebuck and Alexandre (2001).

Papers on other costs of drug use are by Cartwright (1999) on measuring the social costs of drug use, Pudney (2003) on the gateway effect of soft drug use, Fryer, Heaton, Levitt and Murphy (2005) on the impact of crack cocaine, and Blows, Ivers, Connor, Ameratunga, Woodward and Norton (2005) on marijuana use and automobile accidents. An interesting paper on the financial activities of a drug-selling street gang is by Levitt and Venkatesh (2000).

There is also a large literature on drug enforcement policy. There are three particular groups of researchers, however, who have established a substantial body of work in this particular subfield. The first group, centered around the work by Jeffrey Miron, typically is critical of drug prohibition, as represented by Miron (1999, 2001, 2003a, b) and Miron and Zwiebel (1995). The second group, including Bruce Benson and David Rasmussen, is also critical of prohibition and skeptical of the incentives of policy officials in waging the war on drugs, as represented by Benson, Kim, Rasmussen and Zuehlke (1992), Benson, Rasmussen and Kim (1998), Benson and Rasmussen (1998), Mast, Benson and Rasmussen (2000), and Rasmussen and Benson (2003). The third group, including Jonathan Caulkins and Peter Reuter, offers thoughtful papers on the role of research in dealing with the drug problem, and emphasizes the policy distinction between drug harm reduction and drug use reduction, as represented by Caulkins and Reuter (1997), Caulkins, Dworak, Feichtinger and Tragler (2000), Reuter (2001), Caulkins, Reuter, Iguchi and Chiesa (2005), Reuter and Pollack (2006), Reuter (2006), and Caulkins, Reuter and Taylor (2006).

Other papers on drug enforcement policy are by Stevenson (1990), Lee (1993), Brumm and Cloninger (1995), Resignato (2000), Grossman, Chaloupka and Shim (2002), Kuziemko and Levitt (2004) on imprisoning drug offenders, Shepherd and Blackley (2005), and Becker, Murphy and Grossman (2006) on controlling consumption of an illegal good.

8 Social reforms and crime deterrence

Although the core body of economic research on crime focuses on the costs and benefits of traditional deterrence policies that affect the certainty and severity of punishment, there is a substantial and growing literature on other policy options to reduce the crime rate. Along with scholars in other fields, especially criminology, economists have examined the effect of labor market conditions, education, juvenile behavior, family background, and so on, on crime rates. As mentioned previously throughout this book, every dollar spent on one policy option is a dollar less that can be spent on another option. It is important, then, to consider a wide variety of policy options when assessing the pros and cons of any single one. In this chapter, I review several studies that examine alternative social policies that can reduce the crime rate.

Unemployment and crime

One of the fundamental principles of rational crime analysis is that the rational criminal's *choice* to commit crime reveals a preference toward illegal activities over legal ones, such as choosing to enter the legitimate labor market. This principle lends itself well to a simple prediction: in periods of high unemployment, the crime rate will be higher than in periods of low unemployment. If this is true, a possible effective policy to deter crime will be to attempt to improve job opportunities to encourage criminals to choose legitimate employment over illegitimate activities. But, simple as the prediction appears to be, the empirical evidence confirming the direct relationship between crime and unemployment has not been overly persuasive.

Sorting out the effect of unemployment on crime can be difficult to do for several reasons. There may be other factors that affect the crime rate that are themselves affected by the state of the economy. For example, there is evidence to suggest (Ruhm, 1995) that alcohol consumption is *inversely* related to unemployment, yet *directly* related to crime. In this case, greater unemployment leads to less alcohol consumption and *less* crime, working in the opposite direction of the simple prediction. The same argument can be made for drug consumption and gun availability. The reason why alcohol consumption, drug consumption, and gun consumption may all fall with unemployment is because of an income effect.

If unemployment reduces the income of individuals who would otherwise consume more of these goods in better times, it may appear that crime and unemployment are inversely related. Furthermore, with declining incomes in economic downturns, there may be fewer purchases of goods that are attractive for criminals to steal.

Another difficulty in empirically identifying the link between unemployment and crime is that there may be a simultaneous relationship between the two. The usual argument is that unemployment causes more crime, but the causation may work in the other direction if more crime causes unemployment. As I have discussed in Chapter 5, individuals with criminal records may have a difficult time finding employment. Also, businesses may be discouraged from locating in areas with high crime rates. Thus, more crime may lead to more unemployment. But even if researchers can sort out the simultaneity problem, there are other complicating factors that need to be considered.

One other important complication is that legitimate employment and criminal behavior may not be mutually exclusive. It is possible that some individuals continually shift between legitimate and illegitimate activities, depending on the opportunities that exist at any given point in time. Furthermore, being a criminal does not necessarily imply that the individual does not simultaneously hold a legitimate job. In fact, legitimate employment can often facilitate criminal behavior. For example, a drug dealer's customer base may be enhanced with connections made at the workplace. Also, some crimes, such as embezzlement or stealing property from the workplace, require the criminal to be employed. In all, the belief that the relationship between unemployment and crime is a simple one is not likely to be correct.

There are numerous empirical studies that examine the relationship between unemployment and crime, being careful to control for other factors that affect the crime rate (especially deterrence variables). As usual, the studies yield mixed results. One interesting representative study (Raphael and Winter-Ebmer, 2001) examines the relationship between unemployment and two types of crime – property crime and violent crime. Their main result is that unemployment is an important factor in affecting property crime rates, but not as important in affecting violent crime rates. More specifically, reduced unemployment rates reduce property crime rates, but have little effect on reducing violent crime rates. But the reduction in property crime rates attributable to unemployment rates is found to be quite impressive.

Quantitatively speaking, the authors present evidence that, between the years 1992 and 1997 in the United States, the rate of robbery fell by 30 percent, the rate of auto theft fell by 15 percent, the rate of burglary fell by 15 percent, and the rate of larceny fell by 4 percent. During the same period, the unemployment rate fell by 2.5 percent. How much of the decrease in the individual crime rates can be attributed to the decline in the unemployment rate? The authors find that the 2.5 percent decrease in the unemployment rate caused a decrease of 4.3 percent for robbery, 2.5 percent for auto theft, 5 percent for burglary, and 3.7 percent for larceny. Thus, a significant portion of the decline in the property crime rates can be attributed to the decline in the unemployment rate, leading the authors to conclude that improving legitimate job opportunities for potential criminals can be an effective social policy in deterring crime.

Another study (Gould, Weinberg and Mustard, 2002) adds a couple of refinements to identifying the link between crime and job opportunities. First, the authors narrow the link between labor market conditions and the crime rate by considering job opportunities for *unskilled men*. Their reasoning is that unskilled men are the most likely group to commit crimes, therefore it is their job market opportunities that matter as opposed to the job opportunities for the population at large. Second, rather than just focusing on the relationship between crime and the unemployment rate, the authors also consider the link between crime and *wages*. Because unemployment is often short-lived and highly cyclical, the authors believe that wages may be a better measure of labor market conditions to explain the crime rate, since a decline in wages tends to have a longer-lasting impact on individuals.

Throughout the sample period of 1979 to 1997, when the (real) wages of unskilled men in the United States fell by 20 percent, property crime increased by 21 percent, and violent crime increased by 35 percent, the authors find that wage trends can account for approximately 50 percent of the increase in crime rates. They also find that the unemployment rate throughout the period did not affect the long-term crime trend because there was no long-term trend in the unemployment rate. In the short term, however, such as after 1993 when crime rates fell, both improvements in wages and declines in the unemployment rate contributed to the decline in crime rates. Their conclusion is that, to help deter *long-term* crime trends, improvements in the wages paid to unskilled workers are likely to be more effective than improvements in employment opportunities.

One other approach to examining the link between crime and the economy is to look at how income inequality affects crime rates. Compared to the unemployment rate or poverty rate, income inequality offers a different measure of economic conditions. Consider two metropolitan areas with identical unemployment rates and poverty rates (with poverty usually being defined by the percentage of individuals whose income falls below some predetermined level). To whatever extent unemployment and poverty affect crime rates, the effects should be identical across the two areas. But the areas may differ in income inequality, meaning that the *spread* between high income and low income individuals may be greater in one area relative to the other. If the effects of unemployment and poverty are properly controlled for in the regression equation, the potential effect of inequality on crime may be isolated. The simple prediction is that the greater the income inequality the greater the crime rate.

One study (Kelly, 2000) examines the relationship between income inequality and other variables on property and crime rates. Using data from 829 metropolitan counties in the United States in 1994, the author finds that property crime is not affected by inequality in and of itself, but it is affected by other variables such as the poverty rate and police deterrence activity – the higher the poverty rate the greater the property crime rate, and the higher police expenditure per capita the lower the crime rate. Violent crime, on the other hand, does not appear to be affected by poverty or police activity, but is significantly affected by inequality – the greater the income inequality the greater the violent crime rate. The results of this and other studies suggest that not only must we consider other social policy options than traditional deterrence variables in reducing crime, we must also consider the potential distinction between combating property crime versus violent crime.

Imprisonment and post-release employment opportunities

While imprisoned, inmates often have the opportunity to further their education. For an inmate who lacks a high school diploma, a common educational achievement is to obtain a General Educational Development (GED) credential. A GED is typically thought to improve an inmate's post-release quality of life by enhancing legitimate employment opportunities and wages. Compared to an inmate who does not pursue a GED, an inmate with a GED may enjoy better job opportunities for two main reasons. First, preparing for the GED exams may allow an inmate to develop new skills that are valued by potential future employers. Second, even if an inmate earns the GED without developing new skills, the fact that the GED was successfully pursued suggests that the an inmate has innate skills and is motivated to apply them to educational advancement. In either case, the pursuit of the GED is commonly believed to allow an inmate's prison time to be put to good use. Although sound in theory, whether a GED actually improves an inmate's post-release quality of life with respect to job opportunities is an empirical issue.

One study (Tyler and Kling, 2006) examines the impact of the GED on inmates' post-release earning opportunities. Using data from Florida, they present several findings. First, white inmates who earn a GED do not have significantly higher post-release earnings than white (high school dropout) inmates who do not earn the GED. Second, they find a positive earnings benefit of the GED to minority inmates compared to minority inmates who did not earn the credential, but this benefit (roughly a 20 percent increase in earnings) lasts only about two years. And, third, actually earning the GED, as opposed to participating in the educational opportunities but *not* acquiring the credential, has no extra benefit. In all, the GED appears to provide (at best) modest improvements in post-release earnings.

If the GED does not provide improved job prospects, why do inmates participate in the program? One alternative explanation is that inmates pursue the GED to demonstrate good behavior to the prison authorities in an attempt to receive better treatment or to improve their chances at parole. Also, it may simply be that pursuing the GED offers inmates a distraction from an otherwise monotonous prison lifestyle. But even if the GED does not clearly provide better post-release job opportunities, these alternative explanations offer additional benefits of prison educational programs that can offset the costs of such programs.

While one benefit of increased prison sentences is that they can enhance the deterrent effect against crime, there may be an offsetting down side to lengthy incarceration periods. If an inmate's ability to secure post-release employment is negatively related to the incarceration length, successful integration into the legitimate labor market may be difficult to achieve. The longer the incarceration period the more likely will the inmate suffer a deterioration in legitimate job skills. Furthermore, a lengthy prison sentence may create a more pronounced social stigma that negatively affects the inmate's post-release opportunities. Overall, lengthy prison sentences may deter crime for those wishing to avoid such severe punishment, but may increase crime from released inmates who find they have few legitimate alternatives because they have been incarcerated for a long time.

On the other hand, lengthy incarceration periods may enhance an inmate's job prospects, or at least discourage future criminal behavior. As discussed above, an inmate facing a long prison sentence may choose to pursue educational programs while incarcerated. And if it is true that in and of itself a lengthy sentence reduces post-release opportunities, the authorities may compensate by devoting more resources to helping the inmate readjust into society. Furthermore, the lengthier the sentence the older the inmate will be upon release, and older individuals are less likely to commit crime. It is also possible that being away from criminal activities for a long time severs ties between the inmate and previous criminal peers. As is often the case, the theoretical prediction of the effect of incarceration length on legitimate job opportunities is ambiguous.

One empirical study (Kling, 2006) addresses these issues. Using data from Florida and California, the study finds that incarceration length has little effect on post-release earnings. Actually, the largest effect found is in the immediate short run (one to two years) after release, where incarceration length is *positively* related to employment rates and earnings, largely because it is during the period immediately after release that authorities do the most to help inmates reenter society. In the medium term, however, no relationship between incarceration length and employment opportunities is found. More generally, the study does not find evidence that lengthier prison sentences negatively impact post-release job opportunities.

Although the studies discussed in this section find only modest benefits of prison education and post-release supervision, the commonsense appeal of these approaches to aiding inmates' reintegration into society motivates much public discussion of potential prison reforms. In 2006, the Social, Health and Family Affairs Committee of the Council of Europe issued a report that outlined a detailed plan for prison reform for the European member states (*Social Reintegration of Prisoners*, Council of Europe Report, February, 2006). Among the committee's many observations and recommendations, are the following:

> Reintegration presupposes that detention is organised in a manner which facilitates a return to normal living and working conditions. This is a long and difficult process and also requires the co-operation of the social, medical and judicial services if it is to be effective. Returning successfully to a life in the mainstream society prevents repeat offending.
>
> Throughout the Council of Europe's member states, prison does not have the desired effects in terms of successful reintegration and is very often an obstacle to former prisoners' prospects and future employment opportunities.

Vocational training and the prospect of stable employment are undoubtedly the keys to successful rehabilitation and the prevention of reoffending, although account must also, of course, be taken of prisoners' past records and personal experience, as well as labour market trends.

Above all, prisoners' needs must be evaluated and co-operation with local businesses organised so that prisoners can work outside prisons and acquire real work experience. This can be done properly with the help of social workers and with the co-operation of firms and their managers and employees.

Governments should therefore play a more active part in helping ex-prisoners to find work. [A] possible solution would be to introduce quotas for employment of ex-prisoners, in particular in the public sector. In Turkey, for example, firms with more than fifty employees are required to recruit an ex-convict.

These recommendations, along with many others issued in the full report, illustrate the Council's devotion to pursuing social reforms that encourage effective prisoner reintegration into legitimate society.

Juvenile crime

One undisputed fact of criminal behavior is that young individuals, especially young men, commit a disproportionate amount of crime. For example, in the United States in 1997, individuals aged fifteen to nineteen accounted for over 30 percent of property crime arrests, yet made up only 7 percent of the population. Similar numbers hold for violent crime arrests. More generally, approximately 25 percent of the U.S. population is under the age of eighteen. In 2005, 15 percent of all arrests involved persons under the age of eighteen. The most common juvenile crime (in a proportional sense) was arson – with juveniles making up 49 percent of all arrests. For some other representative crimes, the juvenile proportional arrest rate was 37 percent for vandalism, 30 percent for disorderly conduct, 26 percent for motor vehicle theft, 26 percent for burglary, 25 percent for robbery, 18 percent for sexual offenses, 14 percent for aggravated assault, 9 percent for murder, and 2 percent for prostitution (Office of Juvenile Justice and Delinquency Program, *Statistical Briefing Book, 2005*).

To account for high juvenile crime rates when applying the economic model of crime and punishment to young criminals, it may be the case that there is a strong deterrent effect of punishment for young criminals, but *actual* punishment levels are too low to greatly affect their behavior. One study (Levitt and Lochner, 2001) calculates a risk–return trade-off juveniles may face in committing certain types of crimes. For example, property crime is a common juvenile criminal activity. Using rough estimates, the authors find that the average return to a criminal for each incidence of property crime is $200, while the average number of days of incarceration per crime is 0.6 days. In other words, a typical juvenile considering committing a property crime is facing roughly a half-day prison sentence for a $200 gain. In comparison, an adult offender considering the same property crime faces an average of 2.6 days of incarceration. In all, a juvenile criminal may find committing a typical property crime yields a decent rate of return, at least relative to other crimes and to an adult offender.

The standard practice, then, of applying differential punishments to juvenile versus adult offenders may be an important contributing factor in explaining youth crime rates. The policy implication here is straightforward – harsher traditional punishments applied to young criminals may be needed. On the other hand, it may be possible to account for juvenile crime by arguing that the deterrent effect of punishment is very weak for young criminals. If this is the case, it is not the low severity of punishment that is accounting for juvenile crime, but it is the inability of punishment in and of itself to affect juvenile behavior. Keeping with the theme of this chapter, if a juvenile deterrent effect does not exist, alternatives to traditional punishments of fines or prison are required to reduce the youth crime rate.

If you don't believe that the rational crime model applies to adult criminals, you are not going to believe that it applies to juvenile criminals. But even if you do place some stock in the economics approach to crime, you may doubt the validity of the model as applied to teenage offenders. After all, how likely is it that teenagers seriously consider the benefits *and* costs of their criminal actions? Having a broad understanding of the concept of punishment is one thing, but does manipulating the probabilities of apprehension, conviction and the severity of punishment affect juvenile crime? Succinctly put: Does the deterrent effect apply to juvenile offenders?

One study (Mocan and Rees, 2005) makes use of an extensive data set that allows the authors to empirically test for several determinants of juvenile crime. The study's primary source of data consists of information obtained from a survey of nearly 15,000 American juveniles, the vast majority of whom were between the ages of thirteen and seventeen when the survey was conducted in 1995. Control variables include individual and family characteristics such as age, race, ethnic background, religion, parents' education level, and so on. County characteristic variables include population density, unemployment rate, poverty measure, racial population percentages, and so on. Finally, county level arrests per violent crime are used as a measure of crime deterrence.

The study's main result confirms the existence of a deterrent effect for juveniles. The authors find that as the violent crime arrest rate is increased, the probability that juvenile males sell drugs or commit assaults falls, as does the probability that females sell drugs and steal. But the deterrent effect of arrest is not the only significant factor affecting juvenile crime rates. The authors also find that an increase in the county unemployment rate also increases the probabilities of some juvenile crimes. Furthermore, parents' education, religious beliefs, and family structure (in terms of one-parent versus two-parent families) also affect juvenile crime rates. In all, the deterrent effect has some bite, but many other factors come into play in determining juvenile crime rates. As far as social policy is concerned, the strongest avenues available to the authorities may be through manipulating the arrest rate and designing policies aimed at improving job opportunities.

An earlier study (Levitt, 1998a, also discussed in Chapter 3), examines the role of manipulating severity of punishment on juvenile crime. As criminals are on the frontier of moving from a juvenile to adult classification, more severe punishments are applied when convicted. The study finds a sharp decline in crime rates as criminals move from juvenile to adult court. The author also finds that juveniles in general are at least as responsive to the severity of punishment as are adults. But while the severity of punishment does offer a deterrent effect, the author notes that it is typically more expensive to incapacitate a juvenile offender relative to an adult one. Furthermore, other social objectives may be important when deciding the fate of juvenile criminals. While less severe punishment may increase the crime rate, there may be public sympathy for juveniles that encourages policy officials to broaden the scope of relevant issues in deterring such crime.

Actually, the Juvenile Justice and Delinquency Prevention Act of 1974 is an explicit attempt of the federal government to assist state governments to prevent and control juvenile delinquency and to improve the juvenile justice system. To be eligible for federal funding, there are four core requirements that states must satisfy. These requirements are (at their most basic, and still currently relevant):

> *Deinstitutionalization of status offenders.* Children who have committed an offense that would not be defined as criminal if committed by an adult (known as *status offenses*), such as truancy or running away, will not be placed in secure detention or correctional facilities.
>
> *Separation provision.* Juveniles must be separated from adults by sight and sound in secure institutions.
>
> *Jail removal provision.* Juveniles may not be detained in adult jails or lockups for more than six hours.
>
> *Disproportionate minority contact provision.* States are required to reduce the disproportionate number of juvenile members of minority groups who come into contact with the juvenile justice system.

While such distinctions in how juveniles are treated relative to adults may reduce the impact of the deterrent effect of punishment in reducing juvenile crime, the distinctions clearly demonstrate the insistence of the authorities to distinguish between juvenile and adult offenders. But allowing for different experiences within the criminal justice system is not the only way for the authorities to implement social policy to affect juvenile crime rates. It is also possible to reduce the likelihood that juveniles become criminals in the first place.

Education as a crime deterrent

Providing educational opportunities to inmates is not the only way to use education to reduce the crime rate. Improving educational opportunities to young people, especially high school students, may lead to reduced future criminal behavior.

The primary theoretical link between increased education and reduced criminal behavior is fairly straightforward – education increases legitimate job opportunities and wages, thereby reducing the financial attraction of illegitimate criminal activities. But there are several other links between education and reduced crime. As discussed in Chapter 3, the opportunity cost of being imprisoned is likely to be higher for individuals who have the potential to earn high legitimate wages. If education is positively related to earning potential, higher education is indirectly linked to increased severity of punishment, reducing the incentive for criminal behavior. Furthermore, as discussed in Chapter 2, conviction in and of itself provides a social stigma that acts as an additional deterrent, and this stigma is likely to be more severe the more educated the individual. Also, education may affect the preferences of the individual, such as making the individual less myopic and less prone to bearing risks. With changing preferences, individuals may be less likely to become criminals.

Empirically accounting for the effect of education on crime, however, may be difficult to do. One problem is that there may be a reverse causation between education and criminal behavior. The usual predicted causation is that an individual with little education is more likely to commit crime compared to an individual who is well educated. But it is also possible that an individual with a propensity to commit crime is less likely to stay in school compared to an individual who is not prone to commit crime. Thus, is it less education that is accounting for criminal behavior, or is it criminal behavior that is accounting for less education? Another problem is that it may not always be the case that there is a negative relationship between education and crime. For some crimes, such as white-collar crimes, it may be that more education leads to more crime, as well educated individuals may have certain skills that facilitate criminal behavior.

Another difficult empirical problem is in sorting out the effect of education on crime from more traditional crime deterrence policy options that increase the certainty or severity of punishment. Because resources are scarce, it is possible that as the authorities devote more resources to, for example, hiring more police or building more prisons, fewer resources will be devoted to education. If this policy trade-off leads to poorer educational opportunities for some individuals, but also to reduced crime, it may seem that less education is leading to *less* crime. Unfortunately, this would not be demonstrating a causal link between education and crime because the crime reduction might be due solely to the policy decision to devote more resources to crime deterrence.

One thorough study (Lochner and Moretti, 2004) attempts to sort through these complications to determine if the causal link between education and crime is as commonly predicted – more education implies less crime. The study finds evidence that more education does reduce the crime rate, as one extra year of high school (statistically) significantly reduces the probability of arrest and incarceration. This finding is likely best explained by the improved job and wage opportunities afforded to better-educated individuals. Furthermore, the study concludes that an increase in high school graduation rates not only has private benefits to the individuals who graduate, but also *social* benefits in terms of reducing the social costs of crime. Quantitatively, the study finds that a 1 percent increase in the male high school graduation rate leads to a $1.4 billion dollar per year saving in the social costs of crime. Another way of expressing the quantitative results is that the social benefits of increased education are approximately 20 percent of the private benefits, leading the authors to conclude that social policy to improve graduation rates may have further-reaching benefits than just improving the quality of life of the graduates.

School and the incapacitation effect

In addition to education improving legitimate opportunities for juveniles, there is another avenue in which education can play a role in reducing the crime rate. Juveniles are required to be in school for a number of hours and days each year. In a sense, then, school may impose an incapacitation effect on juveniles, just as prison incapacitates adult offenders. This suggests that one potential policy option for reducing juvenile crime is that it may be sensible to increase the amount of time juveniles must attend school. There are a couple of empirical studies that attempt to determine if school attendance reduces juvenile crime (Jacob and Lefgren, 2003; Luallen, 2006). Both studies find similar, and mixed, results.

In addressing the issue of a school incapacitation effect, it is important to recognize that, unlike being imprisoned, school is not in session twenty-four hours a day, seven days a week. There are ample opportunities (evenings, weekends, holidays, and so on) for juveniles to commit crimes even if they spend a large amount of time in school. The studies must be careful, then, to consider crimes committed by juveniles when they *should have* been in school but were not, for reasons described below. Furthermore, it must be taken into account whether increased school time only delays criminal behavior but doesn't prevent it. If, for example, the school day is extended by an hour or two, will there simply be more juvenile crimes committed in the evening hours?

Both studies attempt to control for these complications. The first study examines the juvenile crime rate on school days compared to the crime rate on teacher in-service days, that is, days in which students are excused from school so that teachers can have professional development and planning time away from the classroom. Instead of using in-service days, the second study uses teacher strike days as the reason for why students are not in school. For the purpose of these studies, strike days offer one advantage over in-service days – teacher strikes tend to be unexpected, while in-service days are generally announced well in advance. To whatever extent parents can plan for supervision of their children while they are not in school, strike days may be more difficult for parents to adjust to. Thus, when juveniles are not in school because of strike days compared to in-service days, it is more likely that they may be poorly supervised and more likely to commit crimes.

The first main finding in both studies is that school attendance does provide a significant incapacitation effect, specifically in reducing the property crime rate. Not only is there less property crime on days when school is in session, there does not appear to be a displacement effect across other days. In other words, increased school attendance lowers the *total* property crime rate, by an amount between 15 percent and 30 percent. But this is not the only result of the studies, as they also find that violent crimes between juveniles *increase* with school attendance, by an amount between 30 percent and 37 percent. It seems that as juveniles are required to spend more time with each other, violent crimes between them are more likely to occur.

With the opposing results of reduced property crime versus increased violent crime, it is difficult to evaluate the effectiveness of policies meant to increase school attendance. Perhaps the important lesson from these studies is that one way to reduce juvenile crime is to provide adequate distractions to juveniles. For example, in Elgin, Illinois, the Elgin police department compiled data that showed that 30 percent of juvenile crime on school days occurs between the hours of 3.00 p.m. and 6.00 p.m. To help alleviate this problem, state and federal funding was provided to the YWCA of Elgin for after-school programs that included gang intervention, literacy enrichment, life skills coaching, and games. Programs like these, especially when not placing too many juveniles together at one time, may be well suited to reduce juvenile crime.

Crime in the city

It is a fact that crime rates in cities, especially large metropolitan areas, are larger than crime rates in rural areas. One study (Glaeser and Sacerdote, 1999) offers, and then tries to account for, three possible explanations for this fact. First, there are higher monetary returns to committing crimes in urban areas than in smaller cities or rural areas. This can be explained by greater access to wealthy individuals in large cities, as well as a greater density of victims. The authors find that approximately 13 percent to 33 percent of the urban crime effect is due to this greater-returns-from-crime explanation.

Second, it appears that criminals face a lower probability of arrest in a large city than they do in other areas. This is likely due to the fact that in dense urban areas, for many crimes, the police are going to confront a large number of suspects. Depending on how sensitive the crime rate is to the deterrent effect of the arrest rate, the authors find that this explanation accounts for approximately 10 percent of the urban crime effect. Thus, combining the first two explanations, the authors account for roughly 25 percent to 45 percent of the urban crime effect. So what else accounts for the remaining 55 percent to 75 percent?

The authors' third and most significant explanation is based on observable characteristics of urban residents. It is possible that individuals with a high propensity to commit crimes may choose to live in large cities (for reasons other than the two explanations stated above). For example, housing availability or labor market conditions, or the availability of welfare programs, may induce crime-prone individuals to move to cities. Alternatively, it may be that large cities "alter" their residents in a way that make them more likely to commit crime. For example, peer pressure from social interactions in dense urban areas may induce more criminal behavior. The authors include many urban resident characteristic variables in their regression analysis, such as those relating to poverty, race, education, unemployment, and so on, but find only one strongly significant characteristic – the greater the percentage of female-headed households the greater the crime rate.

Unfortunately, the authors have little to say on whether large urban areas attract female-headed households, or whether urban areas *create* more of these family structures, but they do conclude that family structure is an important determinant of the crime rate in large cities. Once again, this suggests that while such traditional factors such as devoting resources to increasing the certainty or severity of punishment may reduce the crime rate, other social phenomena may come into play. What type of social programs may be needed to either reduce the incidence of female-headed households, or to reduce the propensity for members of such households to commit crimes, is an open and difficult question, but, as seen in the next section, the authorities can best approach the crime deterrence issue by considering a trade-off between traditional crime deterrence policies and broader social reforms.

Prison versus social programs

With most social issues, there are several policy options that can be implemented to resolve whatever problems are at hand. In deterring crime, two such options include devoting resources toward the apprehension, conviction, and punishment of criminals, and devoting resources toward social programs, especially aimed at the young, to discourage future criminal behavior. This leads to an obvious economic question: What is the optimal trade-off between devoting resources to each of these crime deterrence options? In theory, the economic answer is to devote resources until the last dollar spent on each policy option brings the same return in deterrence benefits. If, conversely, one more dollar toward punishment (for example) can be more effective than one more dollar toward social programs, if that last dollar isn't allocated toward punishment, the optimal use of resources cannot be achieved. This all sounds very simple, and it is, *in theory*, but in the real world it is unlikely that resources can be optimally allocated across several policy options mainly because it is extremely difficult to measure the marginal value of a dollar in different settings.

One ambitious study (Donohue and Siegelman, 1998) attempts to measure the trade-off between allocating resources toward increasing the prison population versus expanding social programs in the United States. The authors conclude that by cutting spending on prisons and reallocating those savings to social programs, crime can be reduced. In other words, *without* increasing the total amount of resources used, crime can be reduced, suggesting that too many resources are currently (at the time of the study) being devoted toward prison as a crime deterrent. While their conclusion is interesting, it cannot be taken as definitive because of the numerous assumptions they rely upon. But what deserves more attention than their conclusion is their approach, as it provides an insight into how economists attempt to measure difficult trade-offs. It is this approach that I will now briefly outline.

The authors consider two policy options: (1) increase the prison population by 50 percent over the current level (which is in December 1993 at the time of their study) or (2) maintain the current prison population level and spend the saved resources on potential crime-reducing social programs. To evaluate the benefit of the first option, the authors rely on empirical estimates of how sensitive the crime rate is to changes in the prison population. Typically, studies find that a doubling of the prison population reduces the crime rate within a range of 10 percent to 30 percent. Because option (1) considers only a 50 percent increase in the prison population, the expected reduction in crime falls between 5 percent and 15 percent. Thus, if the incarceration rate is held constant, as proposed in option (2), the crime rate is expected to be 5 percent to 15 percent *higher* than it would be with option (1). This provides the authors with an important benchmark – if additional resources saved with option (2) can be reallocated into social programs that reduce the crime rate by *more* than 5 percent to 15 percent, that reallocation can be considered efficient.

The next step is to calculate the dollar value of resources saved by not increasing the current prison population by 50 percent. Taking into account not only the cost of physically incarcerating the inmates, but also their lost legitimate earnings, the authors find that it would cost between $5.6 billion and $8 billion dollars to increase the prison population by 50 percent. It is this amount of resources that can be reallocated into social programs that may help reduce crime. Such programs can include: preschool and early childhood education; family-based therapy; treatment programs for juvenile delinquents; job skill enhancement programs; and so on.

The last step is to calculate the crime deterrence benefits of devoting the additional resources into these types of social programs, and this is a difficult step. There is very little empirical evidence as to how effective these programs are in reducing crime. The authors use what little evidence there is and make a limiting assumption that only *half* of the estimated benefits can be obtained with the additional resources, yet they still find that it is likely that the resources can be used more efficiently to reduce crime if reallocated away from increasing the prison population and devoted to social programs. They are cautious, though, in noting that their conclusion is more sound if prison has only a modest effect on reducing crime, and if the social programs are able to target the highest-risk group of youngsters. Finally, they correctly point out that, from a political standpoint, reallocating resources from prisons to social programs may not be an attractive option for politicians. Increased incarceration tends to have benefits that are seen fairly quickly, but improved social programs, especially those aimed at youngsters, tend to have current costs but benefits that accrue far in the future. Politicians tend to favor programs that they can take credit for while they are still in office.

It is easy to be critical of this study. There are many assumptions underlying the analysis, as well as numerous empirical estimates that are of questionable accuracy, and compounded with each other. But placing too much importance on the empirical conclusion deflects from the true contribution of the study – its approach to evaluating public policy options. Whether you accept the conclusion or not, the questions raised are truly significant. Resources are scarce, and trying to carefully think about where resources can best be used is what economic policy analysis is all about. There is more to policy analysis than just believing that one option is better than another. Rigorous empirical cost–benefit analysis may be difficult, if not impossible, to complete, but it is always a good start to at least identify key trade-offs.

Notes

Papers on the relationship between crime and labor market conditions such as unemployment and earnings are by Grogger (1995), Raphael and Winter-Ebmer (2001), Levitt (2001), Western, Kling and Weiman (2001), Fajnzylber, Lederman and Loayza (2002), Gould, Weinberg and Mustard (2002), Edmark (2005), Spelman (2005), Allgood, Mustard and Warren (2006), Ihlanfeldt (2006), and Imai, Katayama and Krishna (2006). Excellent papers that provide overviews of this topic are by Freeman (1996, 1999), and Bushway and Reuter (2001). Other related papers are by Butcher and Piehl (1998) on crime and immigration, and Kelly (2000) on crime and income inequality. The paper by Ruhm (1995) examines the relationship between alcohol consumption and economic conditions.

Papers on imprisonment and post-release employment opportunities are by Lochner (2004), Lochner and Moretti (2004), Kling (2006), and Tyler and Kling (2006).

Papers are juvenile crime are by Levitt (1998a), Levitt and Lochner (2001), Jacob and Lefgren (2003), Mocan and Rees (2005), and Luallen (2006). The paper by Hunt (2006) examines the relationship between crime and teenage births.

Papers on crime and social reforms are by Donohue and Siegelman (1998), and Glaeser and Sacerdote (1999). Other interesting papers are by Sah (1991), Glaeser, Sacerdote and Scheinkman (1996) on crime and social interactions, and Heaton (2006) on the relationship between crime and religion.

9 Conclusion: What economists do

One of the most interesting and controversial studies (Donohue and Levitt, 2001b) in the economics of crime literature since the 1990s raised a simple yet shocking question: Does an increase in current abortion rates reduce future crime rates? And when one of the authors published a best-selling book (Levitt and Dubner, 2005) that highlighted the abortion and crime link, all of a sudden the economic analysis of crime was given national attention. But that attention was often not flattering, as the authors of the study were severely criticized, not only for the results of their study, but for undertaking the study in the first place. Although the abortion and crime link has been well presented elsewhere, I will briefly highlight the results of the study, not so much to discuss the results in and of themselves, but to address a separate issue: What does raising and answering this type of question tell us about economists and their approach to analyzing crime?

Abortion and the crime rate

Consider the following two generally agreed upon facts. First, due to the Supreme Court's 1973 *Roe v. Wade* decision, which legalized abortion, there was a substantial increase in the abortion rate at that time. Second, throughout the 1990s the crime rate in the United States sharply declined. The authors examine how these two facts are linked.

The first link between abortion and crime is that, as the current abortion rate is increased, the future crime rate is reduced simply because fewer people are born. The next link has to do with the demographics of the women who are most likely receiving abortions. Teenage girls, unmarried women, and poor women who are pregnant are the most likely to receive abortions. All of these characteristics, however, also tend to suggest that children born to these mothers are most likely to find themselves pursuing criminal activities. In other words, the demographic variables that most commonly are associated with criminals also tend to be most commonly associated with abortion. Abortion not only acts as a population control, it acts as a population control for groups with very specific demographic qualities.

In demonstrating a relationship between abortion and crime, the study identifies several empirical links. First, it is fairly well established that crime rates are highest for criminals between the ages of eighteen and twenty-four. Due to the Supreme Court's *Roe v. Wade* decision legalizing abortion in 1973, an increased abortion rate starting in the early 1970s should lead to a reduced crime rate starting in the early 1990s. It appears to be an empirical fact that, throughout the 1990s, the violent crime and property crime rates sharply dropped. Second, a few states legalized abortion three years before the *Roe v. Wade* decision, and it appears that these states saw a drop in the crime rate before the other states experienced their drop. Third, the effect of abortion on crime appears to be very strong when being careful to separate out other factors that may lead to a lower crime rate, such as increased incarceration rates, increased size of police forces, and strong economic conditions.

The authors find, with their methodology and data, that legalized abortion can account for approximately *half* the reduction in crime in the United States between 1991 and 1997. This is a striking result, even if it is not perfectly accurate due to the nature of statistical research. And other studies (Foote and Goetz, 2005; Joyce, 2004a, b, 2006) of the abortion and crime link have challenged the authors' initial findings. But it is the initial finding that has led to a substantial outpouring of criticisms of the much publicized study, such as the following:

> [This study] is so fraught with stupidity that I hardly know where to start refuting it. Naturally, if you kill off a million and a half people a year, a few criminals will be in that number. So will doctors, philosophers, musicians, and artists.
>
> (Catholics for a Free Choice (CFFC) website)

> I've seen a lot of farfetched and dangerous ideas passed off as "social research," but none more shallow and potentially malicious than the claim that the drop in crime in the United States can be attributed to legalized abortions.
>
> (CFFC website)

> It follows logically that to really eliminate crime, you simply need to get rid of everybody.
>
> (Ellen Goodman website)

> We cannot abort or sterilize our way into a more tranquil, law-abiding society, and we must speak loudly against "conjecture" that even raises the notion that this is a plausible course.
>
> (Cardinal O'Conner website)

> The idea that it's certain people you kill before they're born that reduces crime is horrific and smacks of eugenics.
>
> (Euthanasia website)

> Might I suggest another avenue of research? Let's determine what conditions lead families to produce academics who have no sense of the sanctity and

dignity of human life. Some early childhood intervention in values education might really pay off.

(Susan Wills website)

The authors anticipated these types of criticism, and in their study offered the following statement of their motivations:

> We should emphasize that our goal is to understand why crime has fallen sharply in the 1990s, and to explore the contribution to this decline that may have come from the legalization of abortion in the 1970s. In attempting to identify a link between abortion and crime, we do not mean to suggest that such a link is "good" or "just," but rather, merely to show that such a relationship exists.

(Donohue and Levitt, 2001b, p. 382)

But even if the authors were extremely predisposed to find the results that they reported, even if they had a hidden agenda in favor of legalized abortion or eugenics, would it really matter?

It certainly may be prudent to be suspicious of empirical results that support any preconceived bias the researchers are known to have, but the bias in and of itself does not *refute* the results. To do that, further empirical analysis is required. *Any* study can be stained with bias. What's most important is to be able to verify the integrity of the data and to be able to replicate the results. Furthermore, are the results robust to different configurations of the data and different statistical techniques? Simply criticizing or dismissing a study *because* of its results is not constructive.

As I discussed in the preface, at its best economic reasoning can be used to identify and measure trade-offs. What anyone wants to do with these trade-offs, from policy officials to the person on the street, is completely open-ended. Also, as discussed before, there are two different issues here. The first involves *identifying* all the trade-offs that are associated with crime deterrence policy. The second involves *weighing* the importance of each trade-off. It is one thing to say that you choose to ignore a particular trade-off, but another thing entirely to argue that one doesn't exist or that it shouldn't even be identified.

In the aftermath of this study, some critics argued that the question raised by the authors never should have been raised in the first place. There seem to be some topics that are taboo and beyond the realm of social science research. I may have my own bias here, but I don't see how *any* question is too controversial to be raised. You may not believe that legalized abortion affects the crime rate based on the available evidence. And even if you do believe the results of the study, you may choose not to consider that particular trade-off when debating the pros and cons of legalized abortion. But to argue that the question should never be raised in the first place makes no sense to me. Actually, pushing the boundaries in the way this study does is exactly what is often most highly valued by economists. I like to use this study as a litmus paper test for people's reaction to economic reasoning.

When I tell most people about this study, their first reaction is to cringe. When I first heard about this study, my reaction was: "Why didn't I think of that?"

Final thoughts

In spending over two years researching and writing this book, my views on the economics of crime have often been challenged and refined. Before I began the project, I certainly accepted the main premise of rational crime analysis that criminals respond to changes in the costs and benefits of committing crimes. As an economist, it would be difficult for me not to accept this premise, at least in theory. And with my reading of the empirical literature on whether there is a deterrent effect of punishment, be it through changes in the certainty or in the severity of punishment, I continue to accept that the authorities can fight crime by devoting resources toward enhanced punishment. This statement, however, needs to be qualified.

I do not know what percentage of criminals fit the rational crime model, and make no claim about the prevalence of such behavior. I do believe that manipulating the expected punishment can reduce crime, but I cannot confidently say by how much. I tend to believe that criminals are more responsive to changes in the certainty of punishment (especially through the probability of apprehension) than to changes in the severity of punishment, but it is with the severity of punishment I feel that I have gained the most new insights.

Although economic theory predicts that monetary fines are the most efficient form of punishment from a resource cost perspective, they suffer from implementation difficulties. But it is interesting to see that shaming punishments, another low resource cost form of punishment, are becoming more prevalent. Prison seems to be an extremely effective form of punishment. Not only does prison incapacitate offenders, some of the cleverest studies I read present evidence that it also deters crime. Although prison is a costly form of punishment to the authorities, further expansion of private prisons (not without their own problems) may help alleviate these resource costs.

Where my preconceived ideas were most affected concerned the deterrent effect of the death penalty. Prior to this book, my belief was that economic empirical research had made great strides toward confirming the deterrent effect. While I recognize that there is a body of literature that finds that a deterrent effect of capital punishment exists, I no longer believe that the available evidence has *convincingly* confirmed or refuted the deterrent effect. I consider this to be one of the most open-ended questions in the current economics of crime literature (along with the role of gun control laws and their effect on the crime rate, a debate which closely parallels the death penalty debate). Fundamentally, the available data on capital punishment appear to be too thin to yield robust empirical results one way or the other. Unless there is a substantial increase in the rates of death penalty sentencing and execution, there may never be enough data to confidently address this issue.

As for the issue of racism, I believe that, if you were to ask a random person off the street if they felt that there was racial bias in the criminal justice system, they would very likely answer yes. But even if racial bias is, and is commonly believed to be, a serious problem, economic reasoning allows us to approach the issue more formally. Many of the economic studies identified potential bias in various aspects of the criminal justice system. At the arrest, bail, conviction, and sentencing stages, the existence of racial bias is difficult to empirically refute. Yet one must be careful not to assume that the bias is strictly against minorities, or that there are no efficiency rationales for distinguishing between offenders based on racial or ethnic factors.

What may be more troubling than the existence of racial bias in the criminal justice system, however, is the lack of any pragmatic solutions to the problem. But this doesn't surprise me. There is absolutely no way of eliminating the personal involvement of police officers, prosecutors, judges, jurors, and other civil authorities who comprise the human components of the criminal justice system. Even if the authorities can design rules of engagement with offenders that attempt to minimize discretionary actions, such actions can never be completely eliminated. For example, as discussed in Chapter 5, even supposedly strict sentencing guidelines were found in one study (Mustard, 2001b) not to be strict enough to circumvent the discretion of individual judges. Finally, how well would the criminal justice system function if all discretionary actions could be eliminated? With vast differences across offenders even of the same race or ethnic background, too little discretion may pose more serious problems than too much discretion.

Where my preconceived ideas were least affected concerned the legalization of drugs debate. I've always had a tough time accepting paternalistic arguments advocating social policy to protect people from themselves. The rational addiction model makes sense to me, even though I accept that not all addicts are rational in the way the model depicts. Furthermore, I find the new research on self-control problems and individual demand for drug control policies intriguing, but I have not yet fully embraced that line of thinking. I find it encouraging, however, that economists are continuing to push the boundaries of the rational versus irrational individual behavior assumption.

Where drug use poses the greatest social concern is when users impose external costs on others, such as through increased crime, reduced worker productivity, increased health care costs, and so on. But it also seems clear that many of the social costs of drug use can be *attributed* to the war on drugs itself. Pushing drugs into the underground economy creates a culture of violence associated with their production, distribution, and use. Furthermore, apprehending, convicting, and especially punishing drug-related offenders require a severe commitment of resources from the authorities, and create ample opportunities for potential corruption. Perhaps enhanced treatment programs for users may be a worthwhile pursuit, and legalization may also improve the situation. In the end, I still hold my prior belief about the drug issue: even if drug use imposes a substantial cost on society, there's yet to be an obviously efficient or effective way of dealing with the problem.

Finally, before this project I was unfamiliar with the economic literature on social reforms as alternatives to more traditional crime deterrence policies.

I am pleased to see that economists are expanding their research along these lines, and providing careful consideration of a wide variety of policy options for the authorities to consider. The economic approach to crime does not have to be completely at odds with other disciplines, and this literature in particular demonstrates the usefulness of a multidisciplinary approach to public policy issues.

When I teach my public policy courses, I have no interest in convincing my students to accept economic reasoning. My only interest is in teaching them what economic reasoning entails, and how it can be applied to social issues such as those discussed throughout this book. At the end of the course, if they choose to reject economic reasoning, I hope it is at least with an understanding of why they are rejecting it. Economists bring some interesting ideas into the mix of public policy debate. I believe that this can only make such debate more productive.

Notes

The controversial paper on abortion and the crime rate is by Donohue and Levitt (2001b). Papers critical of that work are by Joyce (2004a, b, 2006) and Foote and Goetz (2005). But also see the replies by Donohue and Levitt (2003, 2006). The phenomenally popular book *Freakonomics* by Levitt and Dubner (2005) provides an accessible discussion of the topic. Also, Levitt (2004) provides an excellent discussion of the abortion and several other economic of crime issues.

My previous book (Winter, 2005), provides a more general discussion of my perspective on the economic approach to social issues.

References

Alexander, C.R. (1999) "On the Nature of the Reputational Penalty for Corporate Crime: Evidence," *Journal of Law and Economics*, 42: 489–526.

Alexander, C.R., Arlen, J. and Cohen, M.A. (1999) "Regulating Corporate Criminal Sanctions: Federal Guidelines and the Sentencing of Public Firms," *Journal of Law and Economics*, 42: 393–422.

Alexander, C.R. and Cohen, M.A. (1996) "New Evidence on the Origins of Corporate Crime," *Managerial and Decision Economics*, 17: 421–435.

Alexander, C.R. and Cohen, M.A. (1999) "Why do Corporations become Criminals? Ownership, Hidden Actions, and Crime as an Agency Cost," *Journal of Corporate Finance*, 5: 1–34.

Allgood, S., Mustard, D.B. and Warren, R.S., Jr. (2006) "The Impact of Youth Criminal Behavior on Adult Earnings," Working Paper.

Alschuler, A.W. (1997) "Two Guns, Four Guns, Six Guns, More Guns: Does Arming the Public Reduce Crime?" *Valparaiso University Law Review*, 31: 365–373.

Andreoni, J. (1991) "Reasonable Doubt and the Optimal Magnitude of Fines: Should the Penalty fit the Crime?" *RAND Journal of Economics*, 22: 385–395.

Antonovics, K.L. and Knight, B.G. (2004) "A New Look at Racial Profiling: Evidence from the Boston Police Department," NBER Working Paper 10634.

Anwar, S. and Fang, H. (2006) "An Alternative Test of Racial Prejudice in Motor Vehicle Searches: Theory and Evidence," *American Economic Review*, 96: 127–151.

Argys, L.M. and Mocan, H.N. (2004) "Who Shall Live and Who Shall Die? An Analysis of Prisoners on Death Row in the United States," *Journal of Legal Studies*, 33: 255–282.

Atkins, R.A. and Rubin, P.H. (2003) "Effects of Criminal Procedure on Crime Rates: Mapping out the Consequences of the Exclusionary Rule," *Journal of Law and Economics*, 46: 157–179.

Avio, K.L. (2000) "The Economics of Prisons," in B. Bouckaert and G. De Geest (eds) *Encyclopedia of Law and Economics*, V. *The Economics of Crime and Litigation*, Cheltenham: Edward Elgar.

Ayres, I. and Donohue, J.J., III (1999) "Nondiscretionary Concealed Weapons Laws: A Case Study of Statistics, Standards of Proof, and Public Policy," *American Law and Economics Review*, 1: 436–470.

Ayres, I. and Donohue, J.J., III (2003a) "Shooting down the 'More Guns Less Crime' Hypothesis," *Stanford Law Review*, 55: 1193–1305.

Ayres, I. and Donohue, J.J., III (2003b) "The Latest Misfires in Support of the 'More Guns, Less Crime' Hypothesis," *Stanford Law Review*, 55: 1371–1398.

Ayres, I. and Levitt, S.D. (1998) "Measuring Positive Externalities from Unobservable Victim Precaution: An Empirical Analysis of Lojack," *Quarterly Journal of Economics*, 113: 43–77.

Ayres, I. and Waldfogel, J. (1994) "A Market Test for Race Discrimination in Bail Setting," *Stanford Law Review*, 46: 987–1047.

Baldus, D.C. and Woodworth, G. (2004) "Race Discrimination and the Legitimacy of Capital Punishment: Reflections on the Interaction of Fact and Perception," *DePaul Law Review*, 53: 1411–1496.

Bar-Gill, O. and Harel, A. (2001) "Crime Rates and Expected Sanctions: The Economics of Deterrence Revisited," *Journal of Legal Studies*, 30: 485–501.

Bartel, A.P. (1975) "An Analysis of Firm Demand for Protection against Crime," *Journal of Legal Studies*, 4: 443–478.

Bartley, W.A. (1999) "Will Rationing Guns Reduce Crime?" *Economics Letters*, 62: 241–243.

Bayer, P. and Pozen, D.E. (2005) "The Effectiveness of Juvenile Correctional Facilities: Public versus Private Management," *Journal of Law and Economics*, 48: 549–589.

Beck, P.W. and Daly, P.A. (1999) "State Constitutional Analysis of Pretext Stops: Racial Profiling and Public Policy Concerns," *Temple Law Review*, 72: 597–618.

Becker, G.S. (1968) "Crime and Punishment: An Economic Approach," *Journal of Political Economy*, 76: 169–217.

Becker, G.S. and Murphy, K.M. (1988) "A Theory of Rational Addiction," *Journal of Political Economy*, 96: 675–700.

Becker, G.S., Murphy, K.M. and Grossman, M. (2006) "The Market for Illegal Goods: The Case of Drugs," *Journal of Political Economy*, 114: 38–60.

Ben-Shahar, O. and Harel, A. (1995) "Blaming the Victim: Optimal Incentives for Private Precautions against Crime," *Journal of Law, Economics, and Organization*, 11: 434–455.

Benson, B.L. (2003) "Do We Want the Production of Prison Services to be More Efficient?" in A. Tabarrok (ed.) *Changing the Guard: Private Prisons and the Control of Crime*, Oakland, CA: Independent Institute.

Benson, B.L. and Mast, B.D. (2001) "Privately Produced General Deterrence," *Journal of Law and Economics*, 44: 725–746.

Benson, B.L. and Rasmussen, D.W. (1998) "The Context of Drug Policy: An Economic Interpretation," *Journal of Drug Issues*, 28: 681–699.

Benson, B.L., Rasmussen, D. and Kim, I. (1998) "Deterrence and Public Policy: Trade-offs in the Allocation of Police Resources," *International Review of Law and Economics*, 18: 77–100.

Benson, B.L., Kim, I., Rasmussen, D.W. and Zuehlke, T.W. (1992) "Is Property Crime Caused by Drug Use or by Drug Enforcement Policy?" *Applied Economics*, 24: 679–692.

Bjerk, D. (2007) "Racial Profiling, Statistical Discrimination, and the Effect of a Colorblind Policy on the Crime Rate," *Journal of Public Economic Theory*, 9: 521–545.

Black, D.A. and Nagin D.S. (1998) "Do Right-to-carry Laws Deter Violent Crime?" *Journal of Legal Studies*, 27: 209–219.

Blows, S., Ivers, R.Q., Connor, J., Ameratunga, S., Woodward, M. and Norton, R. (2005) "Marijuana Use and Car Crash Injury," *Addiction*, 100: 605–611.

Blume, J., Eisenberg, T. and Wells, M.T. (2004) "Explaining Death Row's Population and Racial Composition," *Journal of Empirical Legal Studies*, 1: 165–207.

Bronars, S.G. and Lott, J.R., Jr. (2001) "Criminal Deterrence, Geographic Spillovers, and the Right to Carry Concealed Handguns, *AEA Papers and Proceedings*, 88: 475–479.

Brumm, H.J. and Cloninger, D.O. (1995) "The Drug War and the Homicide Rate: A Direct Correlation?" *Cato Journal*, 14: 509–517.

Buchmueller, T.C. and Zuvekas, S.H. (1998) "Drug Use, Drug Abuse, and Labour Market Outcomes," *Addiction*, 7: 229–245.

Bunzel, H. and Marcoul, P. (2005) "On the Use of Racial Profiling as a Law Enforcement Tool," Working Paper.

Burgess, S.M. and Propper, C. (1998) "Early Health-related Behaviours and their Impact on later Life Chances: Evidence from the U.S.," *Health Economics*, 7: 381–399.

Bushway, S. and Reuter, P. (2001) "Labor Markets and Crime," in J. Wilson and J. Petersilia (eds) *Crime*, second edition, Oakland, CA: ICS Press.

Butcher, K.F. and Piehl, A.M. (1998) "Cross-city Evidence on the Relationship between Immigration and Crime," *Journal of Policy Analysis and Management*, 17: 457–493.

Camerer, C., Issacharoff, S., Loewenstein, G., O'Donoghue, T. and Rabin, M. (2003) "Regulation for Conservatives: Behavioral Economics and the Case for 'Asymmetric Paternalism'," *University of Pennsylvania Law Review*, 151: 1211–1254.

Cameron, S. (1988) "The Economics of Crime Deterrence: A Survey of Theory and Evidence," *Kyklos*, 41: 301–323.

Cartwright, W.S. (1999) "Costs of Drug Abuse to Society," *Journal of Mental Health Policy and Economics*, 2: 133–134.

Caulkins, J.P. (1995) "Domestic Geographic Variation in Illicit Drug Prices," *Journal of Urban Economics*, 37: 38–56.

Caulkins, J.P., Dworak, M., Feichtinger, G. and Tragler, G. (2000) "Price-raising Drug Enforcement and Property Crime: A Dynamic Model," *Journal of Economics*, 71: 227–253.

Caulkins, J.P. and Reuter, P. (1996) "The Meaning and Utility of Drug Prices," *Addiction*, 91: 1261–1264.

Caulkins, J.P. and Reuter, P. (1997) "Setting Goals for Drug Policy: Harm Reduction or Use Reduction?" *Addiction*, 92: 1143–1150.

Caulkins, J.P. and Reuter, P. (1998) "What Price Data tell Us about Drug Markets," *Journal of Drug Issues*, 28: 593–612.

Caulkins, J.P., Reuter, P., Iguchi, M.Y. and Chiesa, J. (2005) "How Goes the War on Drugs? An Assessment of U.S. Drug Problems and Policy," RAND, Drug Policy Research Center.

Caulkins, J.P., Reuter, P. and Taylor, L.J. (2006) "Can Supply Restrictions Lower Price? Violence, Drug Dealing and Positional Advantage," *Contributions to Economic Analysis and Policy*, 5: 1–18.

Chaudhri, V. and Geanakoplos, J. (1998) "A Note on the Economic Rationalization of Gun Control," *Economics Letters*, 58: 51–53.

Chen, M.K. and Shapiro, J.M. (2006) "Does Prison Harden Inmates? A Discontinuity-based Approach," Working Paper.

Close, B.R. and Mason, P.L. (2006) "After the Traffic Stops: Officer Characteristics and Enforcement Actions," *Topics in Economic Analysis and Policy*, 6: 1–41.

Cohen, M.A. (1996) "Theories of Punishment and Empirical Trends in Corporate Criminal Sanctions," *Managerial and Decision Economics*, 17: 399–411.

Cohen, M.A. (2005) *The Costs of Crime and Justice*, New York: Routledge.

Cook, P.J. and Leitzel, J.A. (1996) "'Perversity, Futility, Jeopardy': An Economic Analysis of the Attack on Gun Control," *Law and Contemporary Problems*, 59: 91–118.

Cook, P.J. and Leitzel, J.A. (2002) "'Smart' Guns: A Technological Fix for Regulating the Secondary Market," *Contemporary Economic Policy*, 20: 38–49.

Cook, P.J. and Ludwig, J. (2002) "The Effects of Gun Prevalence on Burglary: Deterrence vs. Inducement," NBER Working Paper 8926.

Cook, P.J. and Ludwig, J. (2004a) "The Social Costs of Gun Ownership," *Journal of Public Economics*, 90: 379–391.

Cook, P.J. and Ludwig, J. (2004b) "Principles for Effective Gun Policy," *Fordham Law Review*, 73: 589–613.

Cook, P.J. and Ludwig, J. (2004c) "Does Gun Prevalence affect Teen Gun Carrying after All?" *Criminology*, 42: 27–54.

Cook, P.J. and Ludwig, J. (2006) "Aiming for Evidence-based Gun Policy," *Journal of Policy Analysis and Management*, 25: 691–735.

Cook, P.J., Ludwig, J., Venkatesh, S.A. and Braga, A.A. (2005) "Underground Gun Markets," NBER Working Paper 11737.

Cook, P.J., Molliconi, S. and Cole, T.B. (1995) "Regulating Gun Markets," *Journal of Criminal Law and Criminology*, 86: 59–92.

Corman, H. and Mocan, H.N. (2000) "A Time-series Analysis of Crime, Deterrence, and Drug Abuse in New York City," *American Economic Review*, 90: 584–604.

Corman, H. and Mocan, H.N. (2005) "Carrots, Sticks and Broken Windows," *Journal of Law and Economics*, 48: 235–266.

Cunneen, C. (2006) "Racism, Discrimination and the Over-representation of Indigenous People in the Criminal Justice System: Some Conceptual and Explanatory Issues," *Current Issues in Criminal Justice*, 17: 329–346. HERE

Dezhbaksh, H. and Rubin, P. (1998) "Lives Saved or Lives Lost? The Effects of Concealed-handgun Laws on Crime," *AEA Papers and Proceedings*, 88: 468–474.

Dezhbakhsh, H., Rubin, P.H. and Shepherd, J.M. (2003) "Does Capital Punishment have a Deterrent Effect? New Evidence from Postmoratorium Panel Data," *American Law and Economics Review,* 5: 344–376.

Dezhbakhsh, H. and Shepherd, J.M. (2006) "The Deterrent Effect of Capital Punishment: Evidence from a 'Judicial Experiment'," *Economic Inquiry* 44: 512–535.

Dharmapala, D. and Ross, S.L. (2004) "Racial Bias in Motor Vehicle Searches: Additional Theory and Evidence," *Contributions to Economic Analysis and Policy*, 3: 1–21.

DiIulio, J.J., Jr. (1996) "Help Wanted: Economists, Crime and Public Policy," *Journal of Economic Perspectives*, 10: 3–24.

Di Tella, R. and Schargrodsky, E. (2004) "Do Police Reduce Crime? Estimates Using the Allocation of Police Forces after a Terrorist Attack," *American Economic Review*, 94: 115–133.

Domberger, S. and Jensen, P. (1997) "Contracting out by the Public Sector: Theory, Evidence, Prospects," *Oxford Review of Economic Policy*, 13: 67–78.

Dominitz, J. (2003) "How Do the Laws of Probability Constrain Legislative and Judicial Efforts to Stop Racial Profiling?" *American Law and Economics Review*, 5: 412–432.

Dominitz, J. and Knowles, J. (2006) "Crime Minimization and Racial Bias: What Can We Learn from Police Search Data?" *Economic Journal*, 116: F368–F384.

Donohue, J.J., III and Levitt, S.D. (1998) "Guns, Violence, and the Efficiency of Illegal Markets," *AEA Papers and Proceedings*, 88: 463–467.

Donohue, J.J., III and Levitt, S.D. (2001a) "The Impact of Race on Policing and Arrests," *Journal of Law and Economics*, 44: 367–394.

Donohue, J.J., III and Levitt, S.D. (2001b) "The Impact of Legalized Abortion on Crime," *Quarterly Journal of Economics*, 116: 379–420.

Donohue, J.J., III and Levitt, S.D. (2003) "Further Evidence that Legalized Abortion Lowered Crime: A Reply to Joyce," *Journal of Human Resources*, 39: 29–49.

Donohue, J.J., III and Levitt, S.D. (2006) "Measurement Error, Legalized Abortion, and the Decline in Crime: A Response to Foote and Goetz (2005)," NBER Working Paper 11987.

Donohue, J.J., III and Siegelman, P. (1998) "Allocating Resources among Prisons and Social Programs in the Battle against Crime," *Journal of Legal Studies*, 27: 1–43.

Donohue, J.J., III and Wolfers, J. (2005) "Uses and Abuses of Empirical Evidence in the Death Penalty Debate," *Stanford Law Review*, 58: 791–846.

Duggan, M. (2001) "More Guns More Crime," *Journal of Political Economy*, 109: 1086–1114.

Durlauf, S.N. (2005) "Racial Profiling as a Public Policy Question: Efficiency, Equity, and Ambiguity," *AEA Papers and Proceedings*, 95: 132–136.

Dyck, A., Morse, A. and Zingales, L. (2007) "Who Blows the Whistle on Corporate Fraud?" NBER Working Paper 12882.

Edmark, K. (2005) "Unemployment and Crime: Is there a Connection?" *Scandinavian Journal of Economics*, 107: 353–373.

Ehrlich, I. (1975) "The Deterrent Effect of Capital Punishment: A Question of Life and Death, *American Economic Review*, 65: 397–417.

Ehrlich, I. (1977) "Capital Punishment and Deterrence: Some Further Thoughts and Additional Evidence," *Journal of Political Economy*, 85: 741–788.

Ehrlich, I. (1996) "Crime, Punishment, and the Market for Offenses," *Journal of Economic Perspectives*, 10: 43–67.

Eide, E. (1999) "Economics of Criminal Behavior," in B. Bouckaert and G. De Geest (eds) *Encyclopedia of Law and Economics*, V. *The Economics of Crime and Litigation*, Cheltenham: Edward Elgar.

Eisenberg, T., Garvey, S.P. and Wells, M.T. (2001) "Forecasting Life and Death: Juror Race, Religion, and Attitude toward the Death Penalty," *Journal of Legal Studies*, 30: 277–311.

Ekelund, R.B, Jackson, J.D., Ressler, R.W. and Tollison, R.D. (2006) "Marginal Deterrence and Multiple Murders," *Southern Economic Journal*, 72: 521–541.

Elder, H.W. (1989) "Trials and Settlements in the Criminal Courts: An Empirical Analysis of Dispositions and Sentencing," *Journal of Legal Studies*, 18: 191–208.

Fajnzylber, P., Lederman, D. and Loayza, N. (2002) "What Causes Violent Crime?" *European Economic Review*, 46: 1323–1357.

Farmer, A. and Terrell, D. (2001) "Crime versus Justice: Is there a Trade-off?" *Journal of Law and Economics*, 44: 345–366.

Foote, C.L. and Goetz, C.F. (2005) "Testing Economic Hypotheses with State-level Data: A Comment on Donohue and Levitt (2001)," Federal Reserve Bank of Boston Working Paper 05–15.

Freeman, R.B. (1996) "Why so many Young American Men Commit Crimes and What might we Do about It?" *Journal of Economic Perspectives*, 10: 25–42.

Freeman, R.B. (1999) "The Economics of Crime," in O. Ashenfelter and D. Card (eds) *Handbook of Labor Economics*, III, New York: Elsevier.

French, M.T., Roebuck, C. and Alexandre, P.K. (2001) "Illicit Drug Use, Employment, and Labor Force Participation," *Southern Economic Journal*, 68: 349–368.

Friedman, D. (1979) "Private Creation and Enforcement of Law: A Historical Case," *Journal of Legal Studies*, 8: 399–415.

Friedman, D. (1981) "Reflections on Optimal Punishment, or: Should the Rich pay Higher Fines?" *Research in Law and Economics*, 3: 185–205.

Friedman, D. (1984) "Efficient Institutions for the Private Enforcement of Law," *Journal of Legal Studies*, 13: 379–397.

Friedman, D. (1999) "Why not Hang them All? The Virtues of Inefficient Punishment," *Journal of Political Economy*, 107: S259–S269.

Friedman, D. (2000) *Law's Order*, Princeton, NJ: Princeton University Press.

Friedman, D. and Sjostrom, W. (1993) "Hanged for a Sheep: The Economics of Marginal Deterrence," *Journal of Legal Studies*, 12: 345–366.

Fryer, R.G., Jr., Heaton, P.S., Levitt, S.D. and Murphy, K.M. (2005) "Measuring the Impact of Crack Cocaine," NBER Working Paper 11318.

Funk, P. (2004) "On the Effective Use of Stigma as a Crime-Deterrent," *European Economic Review*, 48: 715–728.

Garoupa, N. (1997) "The Theory of Optimal Law Enforcement," *Journal of Economic Surveys*, 11: 267–295.

Garoupa, N. (2001) "Optimal Magnitude and Probability of Fines," *European Economic Review*, 45: 1765–1771.

Garoupa, N. and Gravelle, H. (2003) "Efficient Deterrence does not Require that the Wealthy be able to Buy Justice," *Journal of institutional and Theoretical Economics*, 159: 545–552.

Garoupa, N. and Klerman, D. (2002) "Optimal Law Enforcement with a Rent-seeking Government," *American Law and Economics Review*, 4: 116–140.

Gelman, A., Fagan, J. and Kiss, A. (2006) "An Analysis of the NYPD's Stop-and-frisk Policy in the Context of Claims of Racial Bias," Working Paper.

Gill, A.M. and Michaels, R.J. (1992) "Does Drug Use Lower Wages?" *Industrial and Labor Relations Review*, 45: 419–434.

Glaeser, E.L. and Glendon, S. (1998) "Who owns Guns? Criminals, Victims, and the Culture of Violence," *AEA Papers and Proceedings*, 88: 458–462.

Glaeser, E.L., Kessler, D.P. and Piehl, A.M. (2000) "What do Prosecutors Maximize? An Analysis of the Federalization of Drug Crimes," *American Law and Economics Review*, 2: 259–290.

Glaeser, E.L. and Sacerdote, B. (1999) "Why is there More Crime in Cities?" *Journal of Political Economy*, 107: S225–S258.

Glaeser, E.L. and Sacerdote, B. (2003) "Sentencing in Homicide Cases and the Role of Vengeance," *Journal of Legal Studies*, 32: 363–382.

Glaeser, E.L., Sacerdote, B. and Scheinkman, J.A. (1996) "Crime and Social Interactions, *Quarterly Journal of Economics*, 111: 508–548.

Goodman, J.C. and Porter, P. (2002) "Is the Criminal Justice System Just?" *International Review of Law and Economics*, 22: 25–39.

Gould, E.D., Weinberg, B.A. and Mustard, D.B. (2002) "Crime Rates and Local Labor Market Opportunities in the United States, 1979–1997," *Review of Economics and Statistics*, 84: 45–61.

Grogger, J. (1991) "Certainty vs. Severity of Punishment," *Economic Inquiry*, 29: 297–309.

Grogger, J. (1995) "The Effect of Arrests on the Employment and Earnings of Young Men," *Quarterly Journal of Economics*, 110: 51–71.

Grogger, J. and Ridgeway, G. (2006) "Testing for Racial Profiling in Traffic Stops from behind a Veil of Darkness," *Journal of the American Statistical Association*, 101: 878–887.

Grossman, M. and Chaloupka, F.J. (1998) "The Demand for Cocaine by Young Adults: A Rational Addiction Approach," *Journal of Health Economics*, 17: 427–474.

Grossman, M., Chaloupka, F.J. and Anderson, R. (1998) "A Survey of Economic Models of Addictive Behavior," *Journal of Drug Issues*, 28: 631–643.

Grossman, M., Chaloupka, F.J. and Shim, K. (2002) "Illegal Drug Use and Public Policy," *Health Affairs*, 21: 134–145.

Gyimah-Brempong, K. and Price, G.N. (2006) "Crime and Punishment: And Skin Hue Too?" *AEA Papers and Proceedings*, 96: 246–250.

Hakim, S., Rengert, G.F. and Shachmurove, Y. (1995) "Burglar and Fire Alarms: Costs and Benefits to the Locality," *American Journal of Economics and Sociology*, 54: 145–161.

Hart, O., Shleifer, A. and Vishny, R.W. (1997) "The Proper Scope of Government: Theory and an Application to Prisons," *Quarterly Journal of Economics*, 112: 1127–1161.

Hay, J.R. and Shleifer, A. (1998) "Private Enforcement of Public Laws: A Theory of Legal Reform," *AEA Papers and Proceedings*, 88: 398–403.

Heaton, P. (2006) "Does Religion Really Reduce Crime?" *Journal of Law and Economics*, 49: 147–172.

Helland, E. and Tabarrok, A. (2004) "The Fugitive: Evidence on Public versus Private Law Enforcement from Bail Jumping," *Journal of Law and Economics*, 47: 93–122.

Helsey, R.W. (2001) "Stolen Gun Control," *Journal of Urban Economics*, 50: 436–447.

Hernandez-Murillo, R. and Knowles, J. (2004) "Racial Profiling or Racist Policing? Bound Tests in Aggregate Data", *International Economic Review*, 45: 959–989.

Holzer, H.J. Raphael, S. and Stoll, M.A. (2006) "Perceived Criminality, Criminal Background Checks, and the Racial Hiring Practices of Employers," *Journal of Law and Economics*, 49: 451–480.

Hui-wen, K. and Ping, P.L. (1994) "Private Security: Deterrent or Diversion?" *International Review of Law and Economics*, 14: 87–101.

Hunt, J. (2006) "Do Teen Births keep American Crime High?" *Journal of Law and Economics*, 49: 533–566.

Ihlanfeldt, K.R. (2006) "Neighborhood Crime and Young Males' Job Opportunity," *Journal of Law and Economics*, 49: 249–283.

Imai, S., Katayama, H. and Krishna, K. (2006) "Crime and Young Men: The Role of Arrest, Criminal Experience and Heterogeneity," NBER Working Paper 12221.

Jacob, B.A. and Lefgren, L. (2003) "Are Idle Hands the Devil's Workshop? Incapacitation, Concentration, and Juvenile Crime," *American Economic Review*, 93: 1560–1577.

Joyce, T.J. (2004a) "Did Legalized Abortion Lower Crime?" *Journal of Human Resources*, 39: 1–28.

Joyce, T.J. (2004b) "Further Tests of Abortion and Crime," NBER Working Paper 10564.

Joyce, T.J. (2006) "Further Tests of Abortion and Crime: A Response to Donohue and Levitt (2001, 2004, 2006)," NBER Working Paper 12607.

Kaestner, R. (1991) "The Effect of Illicit Drug Use on the Wages of Young Adults," *Journal of Labor Economics*, 9: 381–412.

Kaestner, R. (1994a) "New Estimates of the Effect of Marijuana and Cocaine Use on Wages," *Industrial and Labor Relations Review*, 47: 454–470.

Kaestner, R. (1994b) "The Effect of Illicit Drug Use on the Labor Supply of Young Adults," *Journal of Human Resources*, 29: 126–155.

Kaestner, R. (1998) "Illicit Drug Use and Labor Market Outcomes: A Review of Economic Theory and its Empirical Implications," *Journal of Drug Issues*, 28: 663–680.

Kaestner, R. and Grossman, M. (1998) "The Effect of Drug Use on Workplace Accidents," *Labour Economics*, 5: 267–294.

Kahan, D.M. (1996) "What do Alternative Sanctions Mean?" *University of Chicago Law Review*, 63: 591–653.

Kahan, D.M. and Posner, E.A. (1999) "Shaming White Collar Criminals: A Proposal for Reform of the Federal Sentencing Guidelines," *Journal of Law and Economics*, 42: 365–391.

Karpoff, J.M. and Lott, J.R., Jr. (1993) "The Reputational Penalty Firms bear from Committing Criminal Fraud," *Journal of Law and Economics*, 36: 757–802.

Katz, L., Levitt, S.D. and Shustorovich, E. (2003) "Prison Conditions, Capital Punishment, and Deterrence," *American Law and Economics Review*, 5: 318–343.

Kelly, M. (2000) "Inequality and Crime," *Review of Economics and Statistics*, 82: 530–539.

Kessler, D.P. and Piehl, A.M. (1998) "The Role of Discretion in the Criminal Justice System," *Journal of Law, Economics, and Organization*, 14: 256–276.

Kessler, D. and Levitt, S.D. (1999) "Using Sentence Enhancements to Distinguish between Deterrence and Incapacitation," *Journal of Law and Economics*, 42: 343–363.

Kling, J.R. (2006) "Incarceration Length, Employment, and Earnings," *American Economic Review*, 96: 863–876.

Knowles, J., Persico, N. and Todd, P. (2001) "Racial Bias in Motor Vehicle Searches: Theory and Evidence," *Journal of Political Economy*, 109: 203–229.

Kobayashi, B.H. and Lott, J.R. (1996) "In Defense of Criminal Defense Expenditures and Plea Bargaining," *International Review of Law and Economics*, 16: 397–416.

Kubik, J.D. and Moran, J.R. (2003) "Lethal Elections: Gubernatorial Politics and the Timing of Executions," *Journal of Law and Economics*, 46: 1–25.

Kuziemko, I. and Levitt, S.D. (2004) "An Empirical Analysis of Imprisoning Drug Offenders," *Journal of Public Economics*, 88: 2043–2066.

Kuziemko, I. (2006) "Does the Threat of the Death Penalty affect Plea Bargaining in Murder Cases? Evidence from New York's 1995 Reinstatement of Capital Punishment," *American Law and Economics Review*, 8: 116–142.

Kwon, I.G. and Baack, D.W. (2005) "The Effectiveness of Legislation Controlling Gun Usage: A Holistic Measure of Gun Control Legislation," *American Journal of Economics and Sociology*, 64: 533–547.

Landes, W.M. and Posner, R.A. (1975) "The Private Enforcement of Law," *Journal of Legal Studies*, 4: 1–46.

Lando, H. (2006) "Does Wrongful Conviction Lower Deterrence?" *Journal of Legal Studies*, 35: 327–337.

Langbein, L.I. (1999) "Politics, Rules, and Death Row: Why States Eschew or Execute Executions," *Social Science Quarterly*, 80: 629–647.

Leamer, E.E. (1983) "Let's Take the Con out of Econometrics," *American Economic Review*, 73: 31–43.

Lee, D.S. and McCrary, J. (2004) "The Deterrence Effect of Criminal Sanctions," Working Paper.

Lee, L.W. (1993) "Would Harassing Drug Users Work?" *Journal of Political Economy*, 101: 939–959.

Leung, A., Woolley, F., Tremblay, R.E. and Vitaro, F. (2002) "Who Gets Caught? Statistical Discrimination in Law Enforcement," Working Paper.

Levitt, S.D. (1996) "The Effect of Prison Population Size on Crime Rates: Evidence from Prison Overcrowding Litigation," *Quarterly Journal of Economics*, 111: 319–351.

Levitt, S.D. (1997a) "Using Electoral Cycles in Police Hiring to Estimate the Effect of Police on Crime," *American Economic Review*, 87: 270–290.

Levitt, S.D. (1997b) "Incentive Compatibility Constraints as an Explanation for the Use of Prison Sentences instead of Fines," *International Review of Law and Economics*, 17: 179–192.

Levitt, S.D. (1998a) "Juvenile Crime and Punishment," *Journal of Political Economy*, 106: 1156–1185.

Levitt, S.D. (1998b) "Why do Increased Arrest Rates appear to Reduce Crime: Deterrence, Incapacitation, or Measurement Error?" *Economic Inquiry*, 36: 353–372.

Levitt, S.D. (2001) "Alternative Strategies for Identifying the Link between Unemployment and Crime," *Journal of Quantitative Criminology*, 17: 377–390.

Levitt, S.D. (2002) "Using Electoral Cycles in Police Hiring to Estimate the Effects of Police on Crime: Reply," *American Economic Review*, 92: 1244–1250.

Levitt, S.D. (2004) "Understanding why Crime fell in the 1990s: Four Factors that Explain the Decline and Six that Do Not," *Journal of Economic Perspectives*, 18: 163–190.

Levitt, S.D. and Dubner, S.J. (2005) *Freakonomics*, New York: Harper-Collins.

Levitt, S.D. and Lochner, L. (2001) "The Determinants of Juvenile Crime," in J. Gruber (ed.) *Risky Behavior among Youths*, Chicago: University of Chicago Press.

Levitt, S.D. and Venkatesh, S.A. (2000) "An Economic Analysis of a Drug-selling Gang's Finances," *Quarterly Journal of Economics*, 115: 755–789.

Listokin, Y. (2003) "Does More Crime Mean More Prisoners? An Instrumental Variables Approach," *Journal of Law and Economics*, 46: 181–206.

Lochner, L. (2004) "Education, Work, and Crime: A Human Capital Approach," *International Economic Review*, 45: 811–843.

Lochner, L. and Moretti, E. (2004) "The Effect of Education on Crime: Evidence from Prison Inmates, Arrests, and Self-reports," *American Economic Review*, 94: 155–189.

Lott, J.R. Jr. (1987) "Should the Wealthy be able to 'Buy Justice'?" *Journal of Political Economy*, 95: 1307–1316.

Lott, J.R., Jr. (1992a) "Do We Punish High Income Criminals too Heavily?" *Economic Inquiry*, 30: 583–608.

Lott, J.R., Jr. (1992b) "An Attempt at Measuring the Total Monetary Penalty from Drug Convictions: The Importance of an Individual's Reputation," *Journal of Legal Studies*, 21: 158–187.

Lott, J.R., Jr. (1996) "The Level of Optimal Fines to prevent Fraud when Reputations Exist and Penalty Clauses are Unenforceable," *Managerial and Decision Economics*, 17: 363–380.

Lott, J.R., Jr. (2000) "Does a Helping Hand put Others at Risk? Affirmative Action, Police Departments, and Crime," *Economic Inquiry*, 38: 239–277.

Lott, J.R., Jr. (2001) "Guns, Crime, and Safety: Introduction," *Journal of Law and Economics*, 44: 605–614.

Lott, J.R., Jr., and Mustard, D.B. (1997) "Crime, Deterrence, and Right-to-carry Concealed Handguns," *Journal of Legal Studies*, 26: 1–68.

Lott, J.R., Jr. and Whitley, J.E. (2001) "Safe-storage Gun Laws: Accidental Deaths, Suicides, and Crime," *Journal of Law and Economics*, 44: 659–689.

Luallen, J. (2006) "School's out … Forever: A Study of Juvenile Crime, At-risk Youths and Teacher Strikes," *Journal of Urban Economics*, 59: 75–103.

MacDonald, Z. (2004) "What Price Drug Use? The Contribution of Economics to an Evidence-based Drugs Policy," *Journal of Economic Surveys*, 18: 113–152.

MacDonald, Z. and Pudney, S. (2000a) "Illicit Drug Use, Unemployment, and Occupational Attainment," *Journal of Health Economics*, 19: 1089–1115.

MacDonald, Z. and Pudney, S. (2000b) "The Wages of Sin: Illegal Drug Use and the Labour Market," *Labour*, 14: 657–673.

MacDonald, Z. and Pudney, S. (2001) "Illicit Drug Use and Labour Market Achievement: Evidence form the U.K.," *Applied Economics*, 33: 1655–1668.

Marvell, T.B. (2001) "The Impact of Banning Juvenile Gun Possession," *Journal of Law and Economics*, 44: 691–713.

Marvell, T.B. and Moody, C.E. (2001) "The Lethal Effects of the Three-strikes Laws," *Journal of Legal Studies*, 30: 89–106.

Mast, B.D., Benson, B.L. and Rasmussen, D.W. (2000) "Entrepreneurial Police and Drug Enforcement Policy," *Public Choice*, 104: 285–308.

McCrary, J. (2002) "Using Electoral Cycles in Police Hiring to Estimate the Effect of Police on Crime: Comment," *American Economic Review*, 92: 1236–1243.

Messinis, G. (1999) "Habit Formation and the Theory of Addiction," *Journal of Economic Surveys*, 13: 417–442.

Mialon, H.M. and Wiseman, T. (2005) "The Impact of Gun Laws: A Model of Crime and Self-Defense," *Economics Letters*, 88: 170–175.

Miron, J.A. (1999) "Violence and the U.S. Prohibitions of Drugs and Alcohol," *American Law and Economics Review*, 1: 78–114.

Miron, J.A. (2001) "The Economics of Drug Prohibition and Drug Legalization," *Social Research*, 68: 835–855.

Miron, J.A. (2003a) "The Effect of Drug Prohibition on Drug Prices: Evidence from the Markets for Cocaine and Heroin," *Review of Economics and Statistics*, 85: 522–530.

Miron, J.A. (2003b) "A Critique of Estimates of the Economic Costs of Drug Abuse," Working Paper.

Miron, J.A. and Zwiebel, J. (1995) "The Economic Case against Drug Prohibition," *Journal of Economic Perspectives*, 9: 175–192.

Mocan, H.N. and Corman, H. (1998) "An Economic Analysis of Drug Use and Crime," *Journal of Drug Issues*, 28: 613–629.

Mocan, H.N. and Gittings, R.K. (2003) "Getting off Death Row: Commuted Sentences and the Deterrent Effect of Capital Punishment," *Journal of Law and Economics*, 46: 453–478.

Mocan, H.N. and Gittings, R.K. (2006) "The Impact of Incentives on Human Behavior: Can We make it Disappear? The Case of the Death Penalty," NBER Working Paper 12631.

Mocan, H.N. and Rees, D.I. (2005) "Economic Conditions, Deterrence and Juvenile Crime: Evidence from Micro Data," *American Law and Economics Review*, 7: 319–349.

Mocan, H.N. and Tekin, E. (2006) "Guns and Juvenile Crime," *Journal of Law and Economics*, 49: 507–531.

Moody, C.E. and Marvell, T.B. (2005) "Guns and Crime," *Southern Economic Journal*, 71: 720–736.

Mookherjee, D. and Png, I.P.L. (1994) "Marginal Deterrence in Enforcement of Law," *Journal of Political Economy*, 102: 1039–1066.

Moorhouse, J.C. and Wanner, B. (2006) "Does Gun Control Reduce Crime or Does Crime Increase Gun Control?" *Cato Journal*, 26: 103–124.

Mullin, W.P. (2001) "Will Gun Buyback Programs Increase the Quantity of Guns?" *International Review of Law and Economics*, 21: 87–102.

Mustard, D.B. (2001a) "The Impact of Gun Laws on Police Deaths," *Journal of Law and Economics*, 44: 635–657.

Mustard, D.B. (2001b) "Racial, Ethnic, and Gender Disparities in Sentencing: Evidence from the U.S. Federal Courts," *Journal of Law and Economics*, 44: 285–314.

Myers, S., Jr. (2002) "Analysis of Racial Profiling as Policy Analysis," *Journal of Policy and Management*, 21: 287–300.

O'Donoghue, T. and Rabin, M. (2000) "The Economics of Immediate Gratification," *Journal of Behavioral Decision Making*, 13: 233–250.

Owens, J.B. (2000) "Have We No Shame? Thoughts on Shaming, 'White Collar' Criminals, and the Federal Sentencing Guidelines," *American University Law Review*, 49: 1047–1058.

Parker, J.S. (1996) "Doctrine for Destruction: The Case of Corporate Criminal Liability," *Managerial and Decision Economics*, 17: 381–398.

Parker, J.S. (2001) "Guns, Crime, and Academics: Some Reflections on the Gun Control Debate," *Journal of Law and Economics*, 44: 715–723.

Parker, J.S. and Atkins, R.A. (1999) "Did the Corporate Criminal sentencing Guidelines Matter? Some Preliminary Empirical Observations," *Journal of Law and Economics*, 42: 423–453.

Persico, N. (2002) "Racial Profiling, Fairness, and Effectiveness of Policing," *American Economic Review*, 92: 1472–1497.

Persico, N. and Castleman, D.A. (2005) "Detecting Bias: Using Statistical Evidence to Establish Intentional Discrimination in Racial Profiling Cases," *University of Chicago Legal Forum*, 1: 1–19.

Persico, N. and Todd, P. (2004) "Using Hit Rates to Test for Racial Bias in Law Enforcement: Vehicle Searches in Wichita," Working Paper.

Persico, N. and Todd, P. (2005) "Passenger Profiling, Imperfect Screening, and Airport Security," *AEA Papers and Proceedings*, 95: 127–131.

Philipson, T.J. and Posner, R.A. (1993) *Private Choices and Public Health: The AIDS Epidemic in an Economic Perspective*, Cambridge, MA: Harvard University Press.

Philipson, T.J. and Posner, R.A. (1996) "The Economic Epidemiology of Crime," *Journal of Law and Economics*, 34: 405–433.

Plassman, F. and Whitley, J. (2003) "Confirming 'More Guns, Less Crime'," *Stanford Law Review*, 55: 1313–1369.

Polinsky, A.M. (2000) "The Fairness of Sanctions: Some Implications for Optimal Enforcement Policy," *American Law and Economics Review*, 2: 223–237.

Polinsky, A.M. and Shavell, S. (1979) "The Optimal Trade-off between the Probability and Magnitude of Fines," *American Economic Review*, 69: 880–891.

Polinsky, A.M. and Shavell, S. (1999) "On the Disutility and Discounting of Imprisonment and the Theory of Deterrence," *Journal of Legal Studies*, 28: 1–16.

Polinsky, A.M. and Shavell, S. (2000) "The Economic Theory of Public Enforcement of Law," *Journal of Economic Literature*, 38: 45–76.

Pudney, S. (2003) "The Road to Ruin? Sequences of Initiation to Drugs and Crime in Britain," *Economic Journal*, 113: C182–C198.

Raphael, S. and Winter-Ebmer, R. (2001) "Identifying the Effect of Unemployment on Crime," *Journal of Law and Economics*, 44: 259–283.

Rasmusen, E. (1996) "Stigma and Self-fulfilling Expectations of Criminality," *Journal of Law and Economics*, 39: 519–543.

Rasmussen, D.W. and Benson, B.L. (2003) "Rationalizing Drug Policy under Federalism," *Florida State University Law Review*, 30: 679–734.

Rasmussen, D.W., Benson, B.L. and Mocan, H.N. (1998) "The Economics of Substance Abuse in Context: Can Economics be Part of an Integrated Theory of Drug Use?" *Journal of Drug Issues*, 28: 575–592.

Resignato, A.J. (2000) "Violent Crime: A Function of Drug Use or Drug Enforcement?" *Applied Economics*, 32: 681–688.

Reuter, P. (2001) "Why does Research have so little Impact on American Drug Policy?" *Addiction*, 96: 373–376.

Reuter, P. (2005) "Estimating Government Drug Policy Expenditures," *Addiction*, 101: 315–322.

Reuter, P. and Caulkins, J.P. (1995) "Redefining the Goals of National Drug Policy: Recommendations from a Working Group," *American Journal of Public Health*, 85: 1059–1063.

Reuter, P. and Mouzos, J. (2003) "Australia: A Massive Buyback of Low-risk Guns," in J. Ludwig and P.J. Cook (eds) *Evaluating Gun Policy: Effects on Crime and Violence*, Washington, DC: Brookings Institution.

Reuter, P. and Pollack, H. (2006) "How Much can Treatment Reduce National Drug Problems?" *Addiction*, 101: 341–347.

Ridgeway, G. (2006) "Assessing the Effect of Race Bias in post-Traffic Stop Outcomes using Propensity Scores," *Journal of Quantitative Criminology*, 22: 1–29.

Robinson, P.H. and Darley, J.M. (2004) "Does Criminal Law Deter? A Behavioural Science Investigation," *Oxford Journal of Legal Studies*, 24: 173–205.

Rubin, P.H. and Dezhbakhsh, H. (2003) "The Effect of Concealed Handgun Laws on Crime: Beyond the Dummy Variables," *International Review of Law and Economics*, 23: 199–216.

Ruhm, C.J. (1995) "Economic Conditions and Alcohol Problems," *Journal of Health Economics*, 14: 583–603.

Sah, R.K. (1991) "Social Osmosis and Patterns of Crime," *Journal of Political Economy*, 99: 1272–1295.

Shavell, S. (1987a) "The Optimal Use of Nonmonetary Sanctions as a Deterrent," *American Economic Review*, 77: 584–592.

Shavell, S. (1987b) "A Model of Optimal Incapacitation," *AEA Papers and Proceedings*, 77: 107–110.

Shavell, S. (1989) "A Note on Optimal Deterrence when Individuals Choose among Harmful Acts," NBER Working Paper 3061.

Shavell, S. (1991a) "Individual Precautions to Prevent Theft: Private versus Socially Optimal Behavior," *International Review of Law and Economics*, 11: 123–132.

Shavell, S. (1991b) "Specific versus General Enforcement of Law," *Journal of Political Economy*, 99: 1088–1108.

Shepherd, J.M. (2002) "Fear of the First Strike: The Full Deterrent Effect of California's Two- and Three-strikes Legislation," *Journal of Legal studies*, 31: 159–201.

Shepherd, J.M. (2004) "Murders of Passion, Execution Delays, and the Deterrence of Capital Punishment," *Journal of Legal Studies*, 33: 283–321.

Shepherd, J.M. (2005) "Deterrence versus Brutalization: Capital Punishment's Differing Impacts among States," *Michigan Law Review*, 104: 203–255.

Shepard, E.M. and Blackley, P.R. (2005) "Drug Enforcement and Crime: Recent Evidence form New York State," *Social Science Quarterly*, 86: 323–342.

Sieberg, K.K. (2005) *Criminal Dilemmas: Understanding and Preventing Crime*, second edition, Berlin: Springer.

Southwick, L., Jr. (1997) "Do Guns Cause Crime? Does Crime Cause Guns? A Granger Test," *Atlantic Economic Journal*, 25: 256–273.

Spelman, W. (2005) "Jobs or Jails? The Crime Drop in Texas," *Journal of Policy Analysis and Management*, 24: 133–165.

Spurr, S.J. (2002) "The Future of Capital Punishment: Determinants of the time from Death Sentence to Execution," *International Review of Law and Economics*, 22: 1–23.

Steiker, C.S. (2005) "'No, Capital Punishment is not Morally Required': Deterrence, Deontology, and the Death Penalty," *Stanford Law Review*, 58: 101–140.

Stevenson, R. (1990) "Can Markets Cope with Drugs?" *Journal of Drug Issues*, 20: 659–666.

Sunstein, C.R. and Vermeule, A. (2005a) "Is Capital Punishment Morally Required? The Relevance of Life-Life Trade-offs," Working Paper.

Sunstein, C.R. and Vermeule, A. (2005b) "Deterring Murder: A Reply," *Stanford Law Review*, 58: 847–857.

Tauchen, H., Witte, A.D. and Griesinger, H. (1994) "Criminal Deterrence: Revisiting the Issue with a Birth Cohort," *Review of Economics and Statistics*, 76: 399–412.

Thaler, R.H. and Sunstein, C.R. (2003) "Libertarian Paternalism," *AEA Papers and Proceedings*, 93: 175–179.

Todd, P. (2005) "Testing for Racial Bias in Law Enforcement," Working Paper.

Tyler, J.H. and Kling, J.R. (2006) "Prison-based Education and Re-entry into the Mainstream Labor Market," NBER Working Paper 12114.

Ulen, T.S. (1996) "The Economics of Corporate Criminal Liability," *Managerial and Decision Economics*, 17: 351–362.

Viscusi, W.K. (1986) "The Risks and Rewards of Criminal Activity: A Comprehensive Test of Criminal Deterrence," *Journal of Labor Economics*, 4: 317–340.

Volokh, A. (1997) "*n* Guilty Men," *University of Pennsylvania Law Review*, 146: 173–211.

Waldfogel, J. (1994) "Does Conviction have a Persistent Effect on Income and Employment?" *International Review of Law and Economics*, 14: 103–119.

Waldfogel, J. (1995) "Are Fines and Prison Terms Used Efficiently? Evidence on Federal Fraud Offenders," *Journal of Law and Economics*, 38: 107–139.

Weatherburn, D., Fitzgerald, J. and Hua, J. (2003) "Reducing Aboriginal Over-representation in Prison," *Australian Journal of Public Administration*, 62: 65–73.

Western, B., Kling, J.R. and Weiman, D.F. (2001) "The Labor Market Consequences of Incarceration," *Crime and Delinquency*, 47: 410–427.

Wickelgren, A.L. (2003) "Justifying Imprisonment: On the Optimality of Excessively Costly Punishment," *American Law and Economics Review*, 5: 377–411.

Winter, H. (2005) *Trade-offs: An Introduction to Economic Reasoning and Social Issues*, Chicago: University of Chicago Press.

Witte, A.D. and Witt, R. (2001) "What we Spend and What we Get: Public and Private Provision of Criminal Prevention and Criminal Justice," *Fiscal Studies*, 22: 1–40.

Zimmerman, P.R. (2004) "State Executions, Deterrence, and the Incidence of Murder," *Journal of Applied Economics*, 7: 163–193.

Index

Economics of the Law
A Primer

Wolfgang Weigel, University of Vienna, Austria

There is an ever-increasing interest in the question of how and why legal norms can effectively guide human action. This compact textbook demonstrates how economic tools can be used to examine this question and scrutinize these legal norms. Indeed, this is one of the first textbooks to be based on civil law instead of the more usual common law, situating the study of both private and public law within the framework of institutional economics, with recommendations for further reading and a list of key terms in each chapter. Besides the standard economic problems in property, tort, contract, crime and litigation, areas covered include:

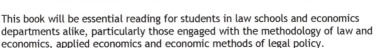

- New Institutional Economics,
- Public Choice,
- Constitutional law
- Public Administrations,
- Regulatory Impact Analysis

This book will be essential reading for students in law schools and economics departments alike, particularly those engaged with the methodology of law and economics, applied economics and economic methods of legal policy.

Contents

Routledge Advanced Texts in Economics and Finance

February 2008
Hb: 978-0-415-40104-3: £90.00
Pb: 978-0-415-40105-0: **£24.99**

Visit www.routledge.com/economics for more information.